Suggestion and Auto-Suggestion

WILLIAM WALKER ATKINSON

COSIMOCLASSICS

NEW YORK

Always map your suggestions on *what you want the children to be*, not what you *fear* they will be, or are. Just as in Auto-Suggestion, you hold the mental image of *what you wish to become*, as a pattern upon which your subconsciousness will model your new character—so should you ever hold before the child a mental picture of that which you wish it to be. Do not misunderstand us—we do not mean to advise *preaching* to the child, no child likes that—we mean to act, and suggest, that the child actually *is* becoming or acting as you wish.

—from "Suggestion in Childhood"

CONTENTS

PART I
SUGGESTION

CHAPTER I.

While the majority of thinking people know what is meant by the word "suggestion," in its modern psychological sense, yet very few of them are able to give even a fairly good definition of the term. And this difficulty is not confined to the general public, for even the writers on the subject of Suggestion seem to experience the same trouble in defining the term, and many of them have seemingly given up the task in despair; for they have plunged right into the middle of the subject, leaving the reader to learn what Suggestion *is* by what it *does*. But, notwithstanding this difficulty, we think it well to begin our consideration of the subject by at least an attempt to define the term, and to give a preliminary explanation of its scientific meaning.

The word "suggestion" is derived from the Latin word *"suggestus,"* which has for its base the word *"suggero,"* meaning: "To carry under." Its original use was in the sense of a "placing under" or deft insinuation of a thought, idea, or impression, under the observant and watchful care of the attention, and into the "inner consciousness" of the individual. The word, as generally used, indicates the use of a hint or other indirect form of calling a matter to the attention of another. But beyond this use, there has arisen a secondary, and more subtle employment of the word, i. e. in the sense of a sly, guarded *insinuation* of an idea, in such a way that the hearer would fail to understand that he was receiving a hint, but would be apt to think that the idea arose in his own mind, from the workings of his own mentality. The word "insinuation" gives one the nearest idea of this form of suggestion. The word "insinuate" means: "To introduce anything gently, or by slow degrees; to instil artfully; to hint guardedly or indirectly; to intimate;" —the main idea of the term being "to creep in." And, indeed many suggestions (in the scientific sense of the term) are so *insinuated* into the mind.

But among psychologists, the word began to take on a new meaning. i. e. that of the introduction of anything into the mind of the other, in an indirect and non-argumentive manner. One of the dictionaries defines this sense of the term as follows: "To introduce indirectly into the mind or thoughts." And, later, psychologists began to use the term in a still broader sense, i. e. that of the *impression* upon the mind by the agency of other objects, such as gesture, signs, words, speech, physical sensations, environment, etc. And this use was extended later, to meet the requirements of the adherents of telepathy, who employed it in the sense of the "insinuation of ideas by telepathic means," the term "mental suggestion" generally being used to distinguish this particular form of suggestion.

The comparatively recent interest in, and discoveries regarding the great subconscious area of mind, caused a new interest to attach to the use of suggestion, for the majority of the writers held that this subconscious region of the mind was particularly amenable to suggestion, and that to this part of the mind all suggestions were really directed and aimed. The "insinuation" was held to be the artful introduction of the thought into this region

of mentality. Many theories were advanced
to account for the phenomena of the subconscious in its phase of the suggestible-mind,
and the discussion still rages. But, no matter
what theory may triumph in the end, the fact
of the existence of the subconscious region of
mind has been firmly established. While the
theorists are disputing about names and generalities, a great army of investigators are
uncovering new principles of application, and
new facts of phenomena regarding this wonderful part of the mind. While the theorists
are disputing about the "Why," the investigators are finding out much about the "How."
The subject has now reached the stage where
it may be divested from mysticism or "supernaturalness," and studied from a purely
scientific position. Subconsciousness without Suggestion, would be like "Hamlet" without the Prince. The two subjects are bound
closely together, and it is difficult to consider
one except in connection with the other.

In order to understand the modern psychological use of the word "suggestion"—which
is the use that we shall make of the term in
this book,—you must make the broad distinc-

tion between the ideas accepted by the mind following the employment of logic, reasoning, demonstration, proof, etc., on the one hand; and *impressions* made upon, or ideas *induced* in the mind by other methods. The words "Impression" and "Induce" will give you the best idea of the effect of suggestion. When an idea is placed in the mind of a person by Suggestion, it is always placed there by one of the following three general methods:

I. Suggestion by means of *impressing* the fact upon the mind by firm authoritative statements, repetition, etc., in which the suggestion acts as a die upon the molten wax; or

II. Suggestion by means of *inducing* the idea in the mind, by indirect insinuation, hint, casual mention, etc., by which the mind is caught off its guard, and the instinctive resistance of the will is escaped; or

III. Suggestion, generally along the lines of association, in which outward appearances, objects, environment, etc., act to *both impress and induce* the idea into the mind.

Of course there are cases in which several of these three methods are associated or combined, but a careful analysis will show that one or more of the three are always in evidence in any and all cases of Suggestion.

To some, the above statements may seem strange, for to many the arguments of a person are held to be the strongest forms of suggestion, impression and induction. But a little analysis will show that there is far more to Suggestion than argument. In the first place mere argument for argument's sake is not a strong suggestion. Men may argue for hours, without any special object in view, and after a great flood of words, all the parties thereto will go on their way, unconvinced, unimpressed, and with no new convictions or ideas "induced" in them, unless under the latter classification may be included the frequent "impression" or conviction that the other party to the argument is either densely ignorant, a fool, bigoted, or else an unmitigated bore. The twelfth juror, who complained of the "eleven stubborn" fellow-jurymen, was not especially amenable to the suggestion by argument; although the same man undoubtedly could have been swayed by the employment of a more subtle form of influence. It is true that often argument is necessary to brush away certain objections to certain ideas, but after that is done the real work of Suggestion is performed by the person wishing to make an impression. As a rule Suggestion is not operated by opposing will to will; argument to argument; or logic to logic. On the contrary, it generally operates by insinuating itself under, over, or around the argument, will, or logic; or else by an authoritative statement, repeated as often as possible, without proof, and avoiding argument. And even where proof or argument is employed, it will be found that the Suggestion is in the form of the main statement, and that the argument and proof are merely the "stage-business" of the performance.

In the form of Suggestion, in which Impression is the method employed, the action is generally direct and open. The "strong men" frequently employ this method effectively, carrying it through by sheer force of personality and real or fancied authority. Where Induction is the form employed, the method resembles that of the diplomat, and tact, *finesse,* and subtle insinuation are the forms of the operation. In this form of Suggestion, which is far more common than is generally imagined, diplomats, women, and others having fine perceptions and instinctive delicacy of mental touch, excel. The lift of an eyebrow; the shrug of a shoulder; the carefully shaded accent—all these are phases of this form of Suggestion. And many little tricks of manner, gesture, etc., are likewise. So common is the use of Suggestion in these times, that an acquaintance with the subject is almost absolutely necessary to every one.

Another form of Suggestion that has sprung into prominence in late years, is that of Therapeutic Suggestion, by which term is meant the employment of Direct Suggestion for the purpose of causing the mind to exert its inherent power to regulate the functions of the body, by means of the involuntary nervous system, etc. Therapeutic Suggestion has reached an important place in the method of combating disease and ill-health, and is now taught in all the principal medical colleges, although until recently regarded by them with disfavor. It also covers and explains many of the various forms of "healing" by various mental and so-called "spiritual" methods, grown so rapidly in popular favor during the past decade. A portion of this book shall be devoted to this branch of the subject.

Another important branch of the general subject of Suggestion is found in what is known as "Auto-Suggestion," which is Self-Suggestion, or Suggestion given by oneself, to oneself, according to certain methods and principles, and which method is also in great favor at the present time, under one name or another, and under one theory or another. Auto-Suggestion may be, and is, advantageously employed along therapeutic lines, and many cases of "healing" by many supposed methods, are really the result of the auto-suggestion of the patient, aroused in various ways. Auto-Suggestion is also very advantageously employed in Character Building, and in Self Development. It is found to be the active basis of all the various forms of self improvement along mental lines.

All of the above forms of Suggestion will be touched upon under the chapters devoted to them in this book, with further explanation and details. The purpose of this introductory chapter is merely to give you a general idea of what Suggestion *is,* and its several forms.

CHAPTER II.

SUGGESTION OF AUTHORITY.

In the preceding chapter we called your attention to the fact that Suggestions are accepted by persons when given by one or more of three general methods. These three methods, you will remember, are: (1) Suggestion by impression, as by authoritative statements, etc.; (2) Suggestion by inducing the idea in the mind, by insinuation, hint, and other indirect means; and (3) Suggestion along the lines of association of outward objects, etc., which act both by impressing and inducing the idea in the receptive mind of the person so suggested to.

But these three classes of suggestion may be considered as being caused by the suggestion reaching the individual along several different lines, or channels. For convenience we may divide these channels of suggestion into five classes, viz:

I.   The Suggestion of Authority;

II. The Suggestion of Association;

III. The Suggestion of Habit;

IV. The Suggestion of Repetition;

V. The Suggestion of Imitation.

In order that you may be able to distinguish the difference between these different phases of Suggestion, we shall call your attention to the details observable in each, briefly and concisely, that we may hasten on to the general subject of the book.

I. *The Suggestion of Authority*: This form of suggestion manifests along both the lines of impression and induction, respectively. That is to say, Suggestion by Authority manifests both in the positive authoritative statements directed to the point; and also by the spoken or written statements made by those who speak or write with an air of authority. It is a peculiarity of the human mind that it is inclined to listen with respect and credence to the words, written or spoken, of persons who assume the air of authority and knowledge. The same person who will weigh carefully every proposition of those whom he considers to be his equals, or inferiors, will accept the statements of those whom he considers to possess authority or knowledge exceeding his own, without more than a casual questioning, and sometimes without any questioning or doubt whatsoever. Let some person posing as an authority, or occupying a position of command, calmly state a fallacy with an air of wisdom and conviction, without any "ifs" or "buts," and many otherwise careful people will accept the suggestion without question; and unless they are afterward forced to analyze it by the light of reason, they will let this seed idea find lodgment in their minds, to blossom and bear fruit thereafter. The explanation is that in such cases the person suspends the critical attention which is usually interposed by the attentive will, and allows the idea to enter his mental castle unchallenged, thereafter to dwell at home there, and to influence other ideas in the future. It is like a man assuming a lordly air and marching past the watchman at the gate of the mental fortress, where the ordinary visitor is challenged and severely scrutinized; his credentials examined; and the mark of approval placed upon him before he may enter.

The acceptance of such suggestions is akin to a person bolting a particle of food, instead

of masticating it. As a rule we bolt many a
bit of mental provender, owing to its stamp of
real or pretended authority. And many persons understanding this phase of suggestion,
take advantage of it, and "use it in their business" accordingly. The confidence-man, as
well as the shrewd politician and the seller of
neatly printed gold mines, imposes himself
upon the public by means of an air of authority, or by what is known in the parlance of the
busy streets, as "putting up a good front."
Some men are all "front," and have nothing
behind their authoritative air—but that authoritative air provides them with a living.
As Bulwer-Lytton makes one of his characters say: "Whenever you are about to utter
something astonishingly false, always begin
with, 'It is an acknowledged fact,' etc." Many
a false statement has been accepted when pref-
aced with a "I assert without fear of contra-
diction," etc. Or, "It is generally conceded
by the best authorities, that," etc. Or, "The
best sources of information agree," etc. Often
there is this variation: "As you probably
know, sir," etc. But in many cases there is
not even this preface—the statement is made

with a "Thus saith the Lord" manner, and is accepted because of the tone and manner accompanying it. As a rule these authoritative suggestions are not accompanied by argument or logical proof—they are thrust at you as self-evident truths. Or, if argument there be, it is generally but a few specious comparisons of bits of sophistry, offered to quiet the mental conscience of the person. Many authoritative suggestions are crystallized into epigrammatic axiomic phrases, which are accepted as true because of their "patness," and apparent smartness, without analysis on the part of those to whom they are offered. Political catch-words, and current explanations belong to this class. Many a phrase is accepted by the public because it "sounds good," without any regard to the truth stated in it.

It would not be so bad if it were merely the acceptance of the suggestion of authority in itself. But that is only the beginning of the trouble, for the suggested idea once admitted to the mind without question takes up its abode there and colors all subsequent thought of the individual. Many of us have experienced periods in our life, when, some new idea

attracting us, we found it necessary to take
mental stock of our other ideas on the subject.
In such cases the majority of us have found
that our minds have been filled with all sorts
of mental rubbish, without any basis in actual
truth, which have been acquired in the past
merely from the acceptance of the suggestions of authority. We are like the man of
whom Josh Billings once said: "He knows
more that hain't so, than any other man
a livin'." We advise you to be a little less
hospitable to these authoritative statements
in the future. Be a little bit more your own
authority. If you find it easier to accept a
strong statement of this kind, at the time, do
so with the mental reservation of "accepted
subject to future examination, with privilege
of rejection." And above everything else in
this line, be sure of the "authority" of your
stater of facts—examine his credentials.

II. *The Suggestion of Association*: This
form of Suggestion is one of the most common
phases. It is found on all sides, and at all
times. The mental law of association makes
it very easy for us to associate certain things
with certain other things, and we will find that

when one of the things is recalled it will bring
with it its associated impressions. For example to many persons the odor of certain
flowers recalls the memory and feelings of
funerals, cemeteries and death. This because
at some time the person has perceived the
identical odor when associated with the scenes
of a funeral. The faint odor of mignonette
will carry the mind back over the years to
some tender episode of the earlier days, and
before we know it we are indulging in sentimental reminiscences and thoughts of "it
might have been" and all the rest of it. The
sound of some old melody will bring back the
feelings, sad or joyful, of time long since past.
We know of a case in which the individual has
a chain of melodies reaching back for many
years, each particular one being connected
with some particular period of his life. When
he wishes to live over the past, he begins hum-
ming, and thus travels from youth to middle-
age, or the reverse, by the sound of the various melodies.

But there are many other forms of suggestion by association. We are apt to associate
a well-dressed man, of commanding carriage,

traveling in an expensive automobile, as a
man of wealth and influence. And, accordingly when some adventurer of the "J. Rufus
Wallingford" type travels our way, clad in
sumptuous apparel, with the air of an Astor-
bilt, and a $10,000 (hired) automobile, we
hasten to place our money and valuables in
his keeping, and esteem ourselves honored by
having been accorded the privilege. The actor,
orator, preacher and politician use the suggestion of association upon us by the employment of tones vibrant with feeling and emotion, which are associated in our minds with
the actual feeling and emotion—and lo! we
are weeping or laughing; smiling or frowning; filled with approval or condemnation, as
the case may be. The speaker pulls the associative strings of suggestion, and we dance
accordingly.

We find that many of our prejudices, favorable or unfavorable, are the result of associations of past experiences. If we have had an
unpleasant business experience with a man
with a peculiar expression or color of hair,
we find it hard to overcome a prejudice against
others of similar personal appearance, in after

years. Sometimes a name will carry associations with it. We once knew a man who would absolutely refuse to have business dealings with any one named "M——," because he had once been badly worsted and cheated in a real estate deal by a man of that name. Many names are associated with persons who had borne them in the past, and, as ridiculous as it may seem, we find it difficult to overcome the prejudice. The majority of people have experiences of this kind.

How many of our readers do not feel an antipathy for some particular article of food, because of some unpleasant experience with that article in the past? Personally, when the writer was a boy, his father wishing to break him of the habit of eating too heartily of "cream-puffs," once offered to pay for all that the boy could eat at one time. Boy-like, the offer was accepted, and the result was disastrous—for years after he could not look at a cream-puff without feeling sad and reminiscent. And the memory of what he once found in a hotel mince-pie, caused an associated suggestion that held its grip with the passage of the years.

How many of our ideas are the result of associated suggestion, we can tell only when we begin to take occasional mental stock. Many of our ideas, feelings, prejudices, likes and dislikes, are the result of this form of suggestion, rather than of anything really attaching to them alone. The moral is that we should watch carefully the company that our mental images are keeping, and avoid unpleasant mental attachments.

CHAPTER III.

III. *The Suggestion of Habit:* This form of Suggestion is closely allied to the preceding phase, i. e. Suggestion of Association, in fact, some consider it to be merely a branch of the latter. But we feel that there is a decided difference in the operation of the two phases, and accordingly prefer to treat this one as forming a separate and distinct phase. Of course, all habit is an association with something in the past, but Suggestion of Habit may arise from an original cause of Suggestion of Authority; Suggestion of Association; Suggestion of Repetition; Suggestion of Imitation; or else from an original decision of the intellect resulting from correct reasoning. The suggestive feature of Suggestion of Habit arises not from the nature of its original cause, but from the fact that the previous action or thought acts as a suggestion for the act or thought of the present. The former act or thought acts as a sugges-

tive "outside influence," although it belongs
to one's own mentality.

It is astonishing to many of us, when oc-
casionally we are brought to a realization of
the degree of habit-action and habit-thought
that has been developed within us. We do
things simply because we have done them before, notwithstanding the fact that the circumstances of the case have altered materially; we think thoughts, and hold opinions,
simply because we have thought so in the past,
although the circumstances may have altered
materially. We get into a jog-trot of habit—
we fall into the rut of routine—and lose initiative thereby. The Suggestion of Habit is
strong with the majority of us.

There is a very good excuse for this development of the Suggestion of Habit, for the
majority of our daily actions and activities are
possible only through having "learned them
by heart." In order to perform our tasks we
must have first learned them consciously, and
with much expenditure of concentrated attention; and then, having learned them, we have
passed them over to the "habit-mind" of the
subconsciousness, that they thereafter be per-

formed automatically, and thus easily. The New Psychology recognizes the important part played by habit in mental operations and physical activities, and therefore urges its students to cultivate the habits which will be beneficial to them, and to inhibit those which may prove detrimental. And it is in this same spirit that we are now calling your attention to the effect of the Suggestion of Habit. We are not advising that you do away with habit —but that you select good habits of thought and action, and then trust to them.

The mind of man is plastic, particularly in youth, the period in which the majority of our mental and physical habits are formed. As Romanes well states:

"No change in childhood's early day,
  No storm that raged, no thought that ran,
But leaves a track upon the clay,
  Which slowly hardens into man."

In our book on "The New Psychology" we have given directions whereby habits may be cultivated, restrained or inhibited, which we shall not repeat here. The realization of the effect of Suggestion of Habit will call your attention to the need of taking account of the same, in the direction of restraint and improvement.

To realize the force of habit, try the following simple tests: Try to put on "the other shoe" first, in the morning. Each of us has the habit of putting on first one particular shoe, in preference to the other. Change to the other shoe, and you will find it awkward, and for some time afterward you will have a subconscious feeling that something is wrong, or has been forgotten. Or, try to put "the other arm" in your coat-sleeve first—each of us has a certain way of putting on a coat, the same arm first each time; and if a change is made the utmost awkwardness is manifested. Each of us gets out of bed on one particular side, and we dress according to rule, in the same way. Try the experiment of putting on a stocking, and then put on the shoe of the same foot instead of proceeding to draw on the second stocking, and see how "mixed up" you will feel. The older we become the more we are apt to become set in our habits of action and thought. We accept the Suggestion of Habit, instead of using initiative, or original thought.

How many people are Republicans or Democrats, as the case may be, simply because they started out so—without regard to any new issues, or local question. They may make high resolves to "do something," but when the election day comes around they fall in line like well drilled soldiers. Many of us belong to certain churches for the same reason—we have just "gotten into the habit of it," and no attraction can lure us to pastures new. We cross the streets at certain corners, on our way home—just because we started out that way. And we hold certain fixed ideas, not because of any special truth or merit in them, but simply because we once accepted some suggestion or statement along the same lines, and thenceforth adopted it as our own, and now "swear by it" as if we had thought it out carefully and intelligently. In fact the ideas that we fight the hardest for are very apt to be those which we have made our own by the Suggestion of Habit rather than those which we have thought out carefully. Bigotry and intolerance, "narrow-mindedness" and mental stubbornness arise largely from this Suggestion of Habit. Sug-

gestion of Habit does not allow the person to
see any "other side" of a question. His subconsciousness has the fixed idea firmly impressed upon it, from habit, and it requires a
mighty wrench to dislodge and cast out the
record. The majority of our ideas are the result of this form of Suggestion. This being
so, it is well for us to take mental stock occa-
sionally, and apply the test of present knowledge and reason to our "inmost convictions,"
the majority of which we would not think of
accepting today, were they presented to us as
new propositions to be examined and judged
by the reason.

IV. *The Suggestion of Repetition*: This
form of Suggestion may seem to be very much
akin to the preceding phase, i. e. Suggestion of
Habit. But there is a marked distinction and
difference. Suggestion of Habit has its power
imparted to it by the habitual repetition of the
act or thought on the part of the individual;
while Suggestion of Repetition gains its power
and force by the repetition of a Suggestion
from some outside object or person. It is an
axiom of Suggestion that: "Suggestion gains
force by repetition." A Suggestion of but

moderate impressive or penetrative power in the first instance, gains force and power at each repetition. It is the old story of the repeated blows of the hammer driving in the nail; or the constant dripping of water wearing away the stone. A Suggestion which passes you without much attention or consideration, when first made, will gain both attention and consideration from you if it be repeated sufficiently often, and in the right manner. Repeated Suggestion tends to break down the instinctive powers of resistance in a person, unless the person realizes that it is a Suggestion and thereupon interposes an obstacle to the impression.

Many things that you accept as beyond question have been impressed upon you by the force of repetition. You hear a thing on all sides, and although you may have no knowledge or proof of it, still you are affected by it, and gradually grow to accept it as at least a presumptive fact. Repeated "they say" has ruined the reputation of many a person. A repeated statement or claim of fact often obtains credence without possessing any basis in truth. Many utterly foolish superstitions and ridiculous "notions" have become current because of repetition. The whole matter is understood when one begins to understand the nature of the subconscious mind, and the region of the memory. In these regions of the mind there is preserved a mental record or impression of each thing that comes to the attention of the person. And these impression-records are strengthened by each repetition of the thing. The realization of this law gives us the key to the development of the memory, and also to the understanding of Suggestion of Repetition. The process and the rule is the same in both cases.

If you wish to impress a thing upon the records of your memory, you know that repetition is one of the most effective methods. Each impression of the die of attention deepens the original record-impression. And in Suggestion of Repetition, each time the Suggestion is made and accepted, the record-impression is made deeper. You have heard the old story of the person who told the tale so often that he grew to believe it himself, have you not? Well, this idea of Suggestion of Repetition is along the same lines. You hear

a thing so often that you get to believe it
yourself—its repetition giving to it an air and
appearance of validity, and causing you to involuntarily imagine that you have always believed it. Who has not known persons who
vigorously combated certain ideas in the beginning, and who afterward yielded to the insistent repeated suggestions of others regarding the thing, until he accepted them and
finally asserted that he had "always so held."

Many a shrewd judge of human nature,
along the lines of salesmanship and advertising, understand this law of Suggestion of
Repetition. They will artfully manage to get
in repeated suggestions, by presenting the
same statements in different terms, or else by
a flat repetition of an authoritative statement,
until you forget the beginning, and the idea
grows to be an old story with you, and one that
you never seem to question. We have heard
of a politician of national renown, who once
said: "Proof? We don't *need* proof! Tell the
public a thing solemnly, and authoritatively,
and *repeat it sufficiently often,* and you will
never need to *prove* anything!" Repetition,
like Pretended Authority are two old frauds

masquerading as Truth. When you once take their measure, you have disarmed them so far as you are concerned. When you call for "Proof," they take refuge in dignity and reiteration—that is their entire stock in trade. But Suggestion of Repetition has its value in imparting Truth. It is a poor rule that won't work both ways.

CHAPTER IV.

V. *The Suggestion of Imitation*: This form of Suggestion while being in itself a distinct phase of Suggestion, nevertheless has a very close relationship with the several other forms of Suggestion. In the acceptance of Suggestion of Authority there is to be found an unconscious imitation of the mental attitude of the person asserting the authority; in Suggestion of Association there is an imitation of the associated thing; and in Suggestion of Repetition there is to be found evidences of imitation. But still, Suggestion of Imitation forms a distinct phase of Suggestion, in itself.

Man is an imitative animal. There is to be found in the human race a decided degree of the faculty of imitation which plays such an important part in the lives of our cousins the apes and monkeys. Many persons who would resent any such comparison, nevertheless evince a constant desire to imitate and follow the actions, thoughts and appearance of those around them. Individuality is a far more rare thing than is generally imagined. In fact, let a man show individuality of taste and action, and he is looked upon as "queer," and is avoided as "out of the ordinary" by the majority of people—unless he is sufficiently strong to force his ideas upon the crowd and thus set the fashion. We live in an era of imitation, notwithstanding our claims of individuality. Our civilization demands that we wear the same cut of clothing; the same width of hat-brim; the same kind of hair-cut, and the same color of neckwear—under the penalty of being called "eccentric."

We copy the attitudes, appearance, tones, and little personal peculiarities of some prominent person, seemingly imagining that by so doing we may absorb his qualities. We think the thoughts of others, and share their ideas, according to the same law of Suggestive Imitation. Ideas, as well as clothes, have their fashion. Our churches and our playhouses fall in line with the examples set them by others who have caught the public notice. There is very little room for the individual who prefers his own ways to those of the leaders of fashion who set the public example—it is "get in line, or get out." Some actress wears a new gown of a striking cut, color, or trimming, and the world of womankind falls in line. Sometimes it is fashionable to be "plump;" sometimes the style changes to the *svelte* willowness of the Directoire gown. The dressmakers and milliners of Paris deliberately coin new styles in order that there may be a demand for the new articles among those who follow the fashions, and the remainder of the people are gradually forced into an acceptance of the arbitrary styles.

A new monarch causes a complete change in the accepted styles of walk, carriage, and personal peculiarities; and even in republics the same thing is being manifested, each president causing a manifestation of the desire to follow the lead in the way of exercise, personalities, etc. An era of calm dignity is followed by an era of strenuousness—an epoch of tennis is followed by one of golf, according to the tastes of the respective leaders. Philosophies, theories, schools of thought and branches of religious denomination are accepted because

The old trick of the practical joker illustrates Suggestion of Imitation. The joker pauses on a crowded thoroughfare, and gazes intently at an imagined something up in the air, or else on the roof of a sky-scraper. In a few moments others stop and gaze upward; then others; and so on until the policemen come to disperse the crowd. We follow the motion of a tight rope walker, swaying in unison with him. We imitate the facial expression of the actor on the stage, frowning or smiling as he does. We catch ourselves imitating the walk or physical motions of persons in whose company we are, and there are but few persons who are immune to the intonation or "brogue" of those with whom they associate. The New Englander falls into the localisms and accent of the West or South if he lives there for a time. The Southerner loses his soft accent when he lives away from home, and is only aware of the change in himself when he happens to return home for a visit, when his folks notice how "Yankeefied" he has become, and he notices the extreme Southern accent among his friends and relatives.

We have a personal knowledge of a young physician, of English-Scotch ancestry (not a drop of German blood in his veins) who spent several years in Germany in the universities and hospitals. When he returned to America he was a German in accent, habits, appearance and tastes. So marked was the change, that he finally settled in a German quarter of the town in which he lived, and practiced exclusively among Germans and persons of German descent, preferring their company and customs, and fitting closely into their requirements and preferences. Contrast the children of foreign parents in this country—see how different they are from their parents in every way. Sometimes the change is an improvement—and sometimes it is a throwing away of the good old qualities and an acquiring of the new objectionable ones. Environment plays a very important part in our lives. And Environment is largely the effect of Suggestion of Imitation—that tendency of the race to level itself up or down; to get into line; to be in the fashion.

Have you ever noticed the contagiousness of mental states, or actions, as evidenced in the daily press. Let there be an elopement, and immediately there are many others of the same kind. Crimes repeat themselves in the same way, even to details. Suicides are suggested in many cases by reading public prints. This fact is recognized by psychologists, and an effort is being made to prohibit the rehearsal in the newspapers of objectionable occurrences. The cheap moving picture shows have come under the supervision of the authorities, because of this fact of Suggestion of Imitation. Young people seeing crimes and other immoralities exhibited in the pictures, display a tendency to imitate them. The stage has a marked effect upon the morals of the people, not in the way of "instruction" as many assume, but in the way of Suggestion by Imitation. This form of Suggestion is attracting much notice from students of sociology and civic progress, and is bound to come to the front during the next ten years. The public has the tendency to follow the suggestions of the things presented to its notice. The remedy is suggested in the evil itself. If undesirable things are imitated, then counteract the evil by prohibiting the same as far as is possible, and neutralize it by presenting the desirable things to the attention in an attractive way.

The phase of Suggestion of Imitation, connected with the health of the people, is also receiving marked attention from the authorities and moulders of public opinion of late. It is recognized that the printing of the advertisements and "literature" of certain patent medicines and other remedies is calculated to react upon the health of the public. These advertisements with their recital of "symptoms," including every possible known physical and mental "feeling," sensation, ache or pain, undoubtedly impress many people with fear and imaginary complaints. This would be bad enough in itself, but is rendered doubly evil by the fact that these imaginary complaints have a tendency to materialize into actual physical troubles, by the effect of Therapeutic Suggestion. Thought tends to take form in action; and Mental Pictures tend to become real in the physical realm. Fear in itself is a powerful depressant, bound to react upon the physical functions and to impair the physical well-being of the person manifesting it. A community may enjoy a very good health record; but flood it with objectionable advertisements and printed matter containing a recital of "symptoms," illustrated with pictures of diseased organs, and in a short time there will be more cases of sickness in the place than ever before in its history. These are proven scientific facts, known to every student of the subject. The moral is obvious.

You will find that the instances of Suggestion of Imitation are far more common, and far greater in number, than those of any of the other forms of Suggestion. This is because the causes operating along these lines are far more common and numerous. There is ever present a great supply of the "raw material" for Suggestion of this kind. The tendency of the race to "get into line;" to "follow my leader;" to act like human sheep or geese makes it easy for them to fall into the habit of accepting these suggestions. You have heard of the custom of sheep to follow the actions of the leader. It is said that if the leader jumps over a rail of a fence, the rest of the flock will follow; and if the rail be removed, the rest of the flock will continue jumping over the place where the rail had been.

In this phase of Suggestion, as well as the others previously mentioned, there is of course the reverse side of the question to be considered. We have shown you how easily people are affected to their detriment, and to the advantage of others who influence them. But it is equally true, and much more worthy of the race, that people may also be influenced for good in the same way. The Suggestion of Authority has its advantageous side, for in this way a worthy strong person or body of people may impose the knowledge of good upon those not so well informed—the crowd will accept it by reason of authority, before their reasons can grasp the "why" of it. In the same way Suggestion by Association may operate for good, providing the associations are desirable. And Suggestion of Habit, and Suggestion of Repetition may become great sources of right action, providing the moving cause is good. And so, Suggestion of Imitation becomes a mighty power for righteousness in the hands of the right persons, and when conducted along the right lines. Those who set good examples, and fashions, influence people just as do those who are at the opposite pole of precept. Good health is just as contagious as disease. When Suggestion of Imitation is well understood by the public generally, there will be a demand for the suppression of the things giving the hurtful suggestions, and for the encouragement and advancement of those setting good examples, and furnishing the right kind of suggestions. The remedy is plain—it is for the people to use it.

CHAPTER V.

In looking around about us for the purpose of gathering instances of typical forms of Suggestion, we are embarrassed by a wealth of material. Instead of having to hunt for such instances, we rather find it difficult to escape the numerous instances of the use of Suggestion which insistently push themselves upon us from all directions. Suggestion is such an active motive principle of human conduct that we find ourselves unable to escape from evidences of its operation, when once we have had our attention directed to the subject. We pick up the morning paper, and there we see hundreds of instances which will work their suggestive influences, for good or evil, upon the minds of those who read them. Here is related the example of some man who has given his life for humanity—and someone will accept the suggestion, and his life will be influenced by the example of this man. Here is related the thieving achievements of some

shrewd hierophant of "Frenzied Finance,"
whose example will be noted and acted upon
by some of its readers. Here is the recital
of a crime, suicide, or scandal, which will plant
its suggestive seed in some congenial soil,
there to grow into action. Here is some inspiring bit of news, which sends a suggestive
thrill through us, and nerves us to higher and
better effort in the day's work. Here is some
depressing item of news, calculated to hatch
forth pessimistic thought and philosophies in
some mind ready for the suggestion. Here is
the speech of some world-worker, in which is
a wealth of inspiring and stimulating suggestion—and next to it is the reverse. And so
it goes, each seed suggestion being extremely
likely to find lodgment in the receptive mind
of persons in harmony with the respective
idea.

And turning to the advertising pages, we
find the same thing repeated. The virtues of
certain brands of Baby Foods, or Pain Killers
are fastened upon our minds by suggestive
notices based upon the principles of Suggestion of Authority or Repetition, respectively.
We are told that "Uneeda Biscuit;" or that

"Ivory Soap Floats;" or that "Puffed Rice is
Shot From Guns;" or that "Babies Cry for
Castoria;" or that "Somebody's Whisky is
Smooth;" or that "Puffer's Cigars are Fra-
grant;" or that "Pilkin's Purple Pills Will
Cure that Tired Feeling;" and so on.

Leaving our homes and entering the street-
cars, elevated trains or suburban expresses,
as the case may be, we find ourselves confronted with startling signs extolling the
wares of various manufactures, each containing some shrewdly worded phrase, telling us
either *to do something* or else that *a certain
thing is true,* in both instances the statement
being connected with certain articles of mer-
chandise.   We gaze upon cleverly drawn pictures of men arrayed in nicely fitting coats or
neat hats, and involuntarily contrast our old
clothes or hats with the pictured elegance, and
thereby set into operation a train of thought
which sooner or later leads us to invest in
some of the articles in question.   These advertisements seek first to arouse desire within us,
and then to drive it home and transform
thought into action, by Suggestion of Repetition.

Leaving our car we find the store windows filled with a suggestive display of attractive things, calculated to arouse desire for posses- sion within our minds. The art of window-display is first to attract the attention by the artistic appearance of the display; and then to arouse desire within us by the quality and appearance of the goods, with a subtle appeal to our bargain instinct by a display of low prices "specially marked down for the Wash-ington's Birthday Clearing Sale." From first to last it is this effort to arouse attention, and to create desire. Look at the crowd of women clustered around the shop windows, gazing longingly upon some attractive display of clothing or hats, or the thousand and one other things so dear to the feminine heart. Don't you realize that out of that crowd there will be some whose "want to" will be so vigor-ously aroused, that the suggestive seed-idea will be sure to blossom into active "must have it" in a day or so?

There are schools for advertising, which carefully instruct their pupils in the laws of psychology in this matter of attracting atten-tion and arousing desire. Do not suppose for a moment that this clever advertising "just happens" to catch your eye, and arouse your desire—not a bit of it. These skilled advertisers, who are paid very large salaries, have been carefully trained in the laws of suggestion, and they put their knowledge into practice every day of the week, with a little extra touch on Sunday. There is one man employed by a large advertising agency in New York and Chicago (he spends part of his time each week in each city, traveling on fast limited trains at night in order to lose no time) who is paid a salary reputed to be equal to that of the President of the United States. And his work, and the value of the same, is along the line of the most clever employment of suggestive words, display, and presentation of the advertisements of the various customers of that agency. Did you think that you bought a certain article because you were convinced from careful examination that it was just what you needed? Nonsense! You bought it because the scientific advertiser had exerted his suggestive art upon you, first by attracting your attention by a striking display of his advertisements, and then by the insistent, and repeated epigrammatic statements regarding the fact that you, yes *you*, needed that particular article. Reason, indeed! You were suggested into it by a series of suggestive pictures and clever phrases. Of course the article is good, and you got your money's worth, but that does not alter the principle.

Then you go into a store, or else a salesman calls at your office. Some of these salesmen, or saleswomen, repel you and you do not care to deal with them. Others have a "winning way" about them, and before long you are placing your orders. Did you suppose that it was just because these salespeople were pleasant, intelligent and courteous? Dear me, you are far behind the times. Of course a pleasant manner, intelligence, and a desire to please have great value in salesmanship, and will always reap their reward in orders and pleased customers—but even this is not always the result of natural inclination, and even if it is, there is more to the thing than that. Do you know that there are numerous schools of salesmanship springing up in all parts of the country, instructing the students in—what do you suppose? In the Psychology of Salesmanship!

Teaching them the psychological laws that are to be found in every sale—teaching them the nature and value of Suggestion in selling goods. And not only this, but many of the large concerns employing solicitors have private courses in salesmanship, in which their salesmen are carefully drilled and trained how to approach people properly; how to present their proposition; how to meet objections; and *how to use Suggestion.* The modern business man has received his education in psychology, and is applying it in his every-day business. We are not objecting to this—personally, we would rather deal with a trained salesman than with a clumsy, untrained, "raw" recruit. We are merely calling your attention to the important part played by Suggestion in every-day business life.

Your day's business takes you into a court room, and lo! you find Suggestion there. You see a witness on the stand, in the hands of a clever lawyer who is drawing out the desired information by a clever line of suggestive questionings. The much decried "leading questions" of the lawyers, which are subject to objection from the opposing side, are but

forms of Suggestion. The up-to-date lawyer
does not need to use the "leading question"—
instead he subtly starts certain trains of
thought in the mina of the witness, by accent-
ing certain words. etc., and thus accomplishes
the same end. Listening to a clever cross-ex-
amination by an expert is equal to a preliminary course in Suggestion. And then, you will
find an employment of Suggestion in the address of counsel to the jury. A sentimental
association is aroused by a reference to something likely to have been experienced by some
of the jurymen; prejudices are aroused by
suggestion and insinuation; doubt is cast on
the statements of opposing witness by a subtle
tone and expression, where words would have
aroused suspicion. And so on to the end. And
even in the judge's charge unconscious suggestion is used. although many judges will in-
dignantly deny this fact. If a judge inclines
toward a certain side of a case, by reason of
his own prejudices or conviction, he will often
unconsciously impart that leaning by suggestion in his charge. This all jurymen know,
and they will tell you that in some way they
became impressed with the true beliefs of the

judge, even although the charge was delivered in a most impartial manner with carefully chosen words. The Suggestion was manifested in the *emphasis* unconsciously placed upon certain facts or words. And, if the case goes to a higher court, on appeal, this suggestive accent or emphasis is missing from the printed words, "if" and "but," which turned the scale in the jury-box.

After the day's work, you start to return home, when you are confronted with a big blinking electric sign, telling you to "Take Home a Box of Riler's Chocolates for Your Wife!" And of course you do. Over the coffee, at dinner, your wife innocently informs you that your best friend has presented his wife with a new set of furs that are *so* becoming; and she wonders if the friend is not an exceptionally able business man to be able to be so liberal; and then he is *so* kind and thoughtful of his wife and family. Thus is the "fur" seed suggestively planted in good rich soil—never fear, it will be well watered with tears, and watched with shy, loving glances, until it blossoms into realization a little later on.

And that night, in your sleep, you will dream of something connected with business that will suggest something else that will have an effect on your actions the next day in your business. You can not escape Suggestion, even in sleep.

CHAPTER VI.

In the preceding chapter we called your attention to the fact that Suggestion is now recognized in the affairs of every-day business life, and that instruction along its lines is now given to those aspiring to reach the attention of the public. Business psychology has come to stay, and it has worked a revolution in many branches of commercial life. Appeals to the public mind are no longer made in a haphazard, hit or miss manner, but along certain well established methods of attracting and holding the public attention, to the end that desire may be aroused and demand created for the wares of the sellers.

Especially is the above so with regard to salesmanship and advertising. It is a fact not generally recognized, that advertising is merely one form of salesmanship—selling at long range. 'And accordingly the "selling talk" of the salesman and the "selling talk" of the advertisement must be based upon the same principles. This fact is recognized by all of the live advertisers and salesmen, and improvement along the lines of selling Suggestion is being made constantly.

In the training of salesmen, there is a constant reference to Suggestion in all of its forms. The embryo salesman is instructed in what is called the "Pre-Approach," by which is meant the general self-training of the salesman, along the lines of Auto-Suggestion, to the end that he may get himself into the proper frame of mind to impress the customer in the best way. The salesman is instructed to fill himself with the idea of the value of the goods he is to offer the customer; the fact that these goods are just what the latter needs and should have in his business; the fact that instead of asking a favor of the customer, the salesman is really doing him a good turn in calling his attention to them—in short, the missionary spirit with its burning zeal for "conversion" is inculcated in the salesman, so that he becomes an enthusiastic advocate instead of a mere "seller of goods." If the instruction in Suggestion went no further than this, it would be a valuable addition to

the qualities of the salesman—but it goes far
beyond this point.

The next stage in the instruction of the
salesman is what is called "The Approach,"
by which is meant the manner in which the
prospective customer should be approached.
The salesman is instructed to carry himself in
such a way as to suggest Self-Respect; and to
dress in such a way as to suggest business
standing and prosperity, avoiding shabbiness
on the one hand, and over-display on the
other. He is taught to maintain a cheerful,
optimistic state of mind, for this suggests itself in his outward appearance and manner
and produces a much better effect on the customer than would a surly, crabbed, pessimistic
manner. Then follows the proper method of
introducing oneself, and one's business, to
the customer, according to the character of the
latter. One of the largest selling concerns in
the country, in its little manual for the use of
its salesmen, says: "The first five minutes of
speaking to a man is likely to make or break
you as far as that sale is concerned. If you
are in any way antagonistic or offensive to
him, you have hurt your chances badly from

the start. If you have failed to definitely please or attract him, you have not done enough.''

Then follow instructions regarding the psychological elements of a sale. First comes Attention—this is the first point in the sale, and the salesman must secure it, or else he can proceed no further. Then follows the stage of Curiosity, or Interest, in which the salesman is taught to arouse the former and gain the latter. Interest must be aroused before desire may be awakened. To arouse interest the business proposition, or article of sale, must be presented in an interesting manner, with well chosen and properly delivered words. This point secured, the salesman is instructed in the science of arousing Desire, for in this lies the motive power which leads to sales. The customer must be made to ''want'' the thing before he will purchase it. Then he must be made to realize that he can afford to buy it. The price is held back until the psychological moment, and then is introduced in a casual way, with little or no emphasis on the amount—just a suggestion that such and such a price is attached to the thing—sort of a side affair, after all. Then comes the point of closing the sale, and obtaining the order or signature. This is the aim and goal of the entire process, and many are the points of instruction imparted regarding this closing. The signing of the order is suggested by pointing to the proper line with the suggestion: "Sign *here*, please;" some going so far as to suggest the action by handing the customer a fountain pen, slanted at the "suggestive angle."

The prospective salesman is trained to recognize the various mental traits predominant in the customer, and methods are supplied whereby these qualities may be appealed to properly. His vanity, pride, covetousness, social aspirations, jealousy, desire for success, desire for advancement, desire for self-improvement—all these are recognized and have their appropriate suggestions. The Imagination is considered, and the salesman is taught how to paint word pictures for it. Salesmanship is indeed a science and an art, in these days, and they are "getting it down finer" every day.

Clerks in retail stores are instructed to have

their customers seated, in order that the
standing salesman may have the advantage of
the "suggestive position." They are also
trained to use the "suggestive question," such
as "This is a very beautiful shade, *isn't it?*"
or "This will make up well, *will it not?*"—the
customer's answer being directly suggested to
him, or her, in the first part of the question,
which consists of a positive statement followed by a question asking for corroboration.
It is much easier to say "Yes!" than "No!"
to such a question—*isn't it?* The saleswoman
who shows her customer an article a little
higher in price than one which is being examined, with the remark: "Now here is something *very* much better. Of course it costs a
little more but it is well worth the difference,
but of course, etc."—the implied suggestion of
the"of course,"to the effect that the customer
might not wish to exceed the lower price,
often acting to put the woman on her mettle,
and she buys the higher-priced thing just to
show that she is "able to" do so. To the
wealthier customers, the suggestion is always
of quality, style, exclusiveness, etc., while to
the poorer it is always "price," "bargains"

and the rest of it. The salesman or sales-woman who understands human nature and Suggestion, will make much larger sales than those who are lacking in this infomation.

The business of window dressing, display, marking prices, etc., makes a liberal use of Suggestion. Models are tastefully dressed in the windows, and the women gazing therein receive the suggestion that they too would look that way, if they wore the same goods. The beautifully formed living model is used to "try on" coats, in the cloak department, that the woman customer may see "just how it will *look on you.*" In the millinery department, the young woman upon whom any hat looks stylish is used to try on the various hats, that the customer may see "how they will look." All this is Suggestion pure and simple—the Suggestion of Association. "Bargain Sales," and "Marked Down" articles are attractive suggestions. "97 cents, marked down from $1.00," suggests a great saving. $4.98 seems so much cheaper than $5.00. Odds and ends of trimmings, unwound and mussed up in a heap on a "Bargain Table" suggest great bargains. The Psychology of the Department Store is a study in Suggestion.

In advertising, the same employment of Suggestion is made. There is the "Direct Command," or Suggestion of Authority which tells you to *do* certain things at once; or to buy certain things for certain reasons. There is the suggestion of taste and flavor in advertisements of eatables and drinkables. "Delicious," "fragrant," "luscious," "sweet," "mild," "invigorating," these and similar words suggest taste, or smell to the reader. Read the advertising columns of the daily newspaper, or the advertising section of the current magazines, in the light of what we have said, and see the ingenious uses of Suggestion. Read the signs in the store windows, or over their doors, and see the part played by Suggestion. "The Store of Quality;" "The Home of Bargains;" etc.,—these are suggestions.

A writer in the magazine "Salesmanship" says: "To make advertising which will sell goods requires development of the human part of the writer. He must realize the different forces which command Attention, Interest, Desire and Conviction." You see then, advertising is salesmanship at long range. The same principles are involved. The same writer says: "The fact is that salesmanship and advertising are practically synonymous terms. A good ad. man must be a good salesman. The only difference lies in the fact that the salesman meets the customer personally, and the ad. man sends him a message in type. The same argument, the same tact, and the same persistence must be present. It takes more brains to sell the goods than it does to make them; you can steal them, but to sell them is an Art." A writer in a magazine devoted to advertising, says: "Really clever ad. writing goes far and away back of, and deeper than, the smartness of phraseology that men like to pay for. . . . Advertising takes into account the subconscious impressions, the varying phases of suggestion and association as received through the eye, the psychology of the direct command,—all worth earnest consideration, and seriously to be reckoned with, however we may balk at the terms." This writer was not afraid to call a spade a spade, and he states a psychological truth. Another writer in the same magazine, says: "Advertising is just salesmanship on paper; a mere money-making means of selling goods rapidly. That 'mysterious something' is just printed persuasion and its other name is 'selling conviction.' Conviction may be imparted *at will* by those few writers who have closely studied the thought process by which conviction is induced. The mission of every ad. is to convert readers into buyers."

The main difference between business arguments and business Suggestion is that the former uses the Broadsword of Proof, and the latter the Rapier of Insinuation—the former appeals to the Reason, the latter to the Feeling and Emotions, and other subconscious mental faculties.

CHAPTER VII.

SUGGESTION AND CHARACTER.

By one's "Character," we mean one's "mental qualities or attributes." Reputation is the opinion that others entertain regarding one; Character is the sum of one's mental qualities and attributes, as they really exist. Character is held to be the result of heredity plus experience and environment. In environment and experience must be included Suggestion. Education is largely a matter of Suggestion; in fact, some leading authorities claim that a man's education is composed almost entirely of Suggestion of some kind. Without entering into a discussion of this question, it may be asserted with safety that a man is largely what he is by reason of the suggestions which he has *accepted*. Remember, we say "accepted," rather than "experienced"—for one experiences many suggestions which he rejects and refuses to accept. The rejected suggestions affect his character only in an indirect way,—

that is in the way of forming a habit of the rejection of similar suggestions. The suggestions which are *accepted* become a part of his nature and character, and may be removed only by suggestions of an entirely opposite nature, strong enough to neutralize the first ones. This being understood, it will be seen what an important part Suggestion plays in the part of all of us.

The suggestions which so forcibly impress themselves upon our characters may reach us along any of the various lines of Suggestion, as stated in the preceding chapters. The Suggestion of Authority is one of the first forms of Suggestion that makes its impress upon the youthful mind. The statements, views, opinions and actions of those to whom the child looks for authority are impressed strongly and deeply upon the child-mind. Acting along with this form is Suggestion of Imitation. The child is an imitative creature, and instinctively "picks up" the ideas, opinions and mannerisms, as well as the general code of life of his elders. The child naturally acquires the impressions suggested to him, involuntarily or voluntarily by those with

whom he associates. He grows to resemble
those with whom he is surrounded. He is
like a sponge absorbing ideas from his associates, particularly his elders, for his nature
is to take in and absorb from the outside
world. The mind in childhood is particularly
plastic, and the habits of his after years are
largely influenced by the impressions of his
early youth. Certain wise churchmen are reported to have said: "Give us the first seven
years of a child's life, and you may have the
rest." And if those first years have been
given to those whose suggestive influence is
undesirable, that child will have hard work to
eradicate the early impressions, in after
years.

Halleck well says: "The analogy between
the plasticity of nerve and brain and that of
plaster of Paris has often been pointed out.
The freshly mixed plaster can easily be
moulded at will, as can a youthful brain and
nerves. Persons after the age of thirty sel-
dom radically change their habits; indeed the
age of twenty finds most of our habits already outlined as they are to remain for life.
The boor at that age will continue to have

boorish peculiarities. Errors in grammar will slip automatically from the tongue. The doctor, the lawyer, the clergyman, the business man, the teacher, soon acquire the peculiar habits of their professions. If we do not get into the right vocation early in life, we are caught in the vise of habits ill-adapted for a change. Our very ways of looking at things have become crystallized. If we put off learning new subjects, we shall remain ignorant of them." While we differ from Prof. Halleck, inasmuch as we claim that The New Psychology has pointed out methods whereby habits may be changed in after life, yet we agree fully with him in his statement regarding the strength of the impressions and suggestions accepted during youth.

But, the effect of Suggestion upon character does not cease with the passing of youth. We are affected by it during our entire life. We are constantly being built up from the Suggestions we accept. If we yield to the inspiring, hopeful, courageous suggestions contained in the words or examples of others, we tend to develop similar qualities in ourselves. If, on the contrary we allow the pessimistic, discouraging, hopeless suggestions of failure, from the words and examples of others, to sink into our minds, we tend to grow in accordance therewith. Our thoughts, ideas, actions and habits become formed from the example and precepts of others, modified of course by our own thoughts on the subject. But even our thoughts and opinions are largely the result of the thoughts and opinions of others which we have *accepted*. Our lives are being modeled from the patterns which we accept from the outside world—therefore we should be very careful what patterns we accept.

It has been often well-said that we are the result of what we have thought. And it is likewise true that we have thought largely what we have accepted and selected from the suggestive influences around and about us. It takes a very strong individual to rise above the effect of his environments, and to shake off the prevailing opinions of his associates and strike out in a new line for himself. Such men are akin to geniuses—the ordinary mortal finds himself incapable of effecting the task, unless he has been inspired to renewed and

scientific effort by the helpful suggestions and
influence of others who know whereof they
speak.   Take a child of the very best heredity, and place it among the thieves of White-
chapel, where it has constantly set for it the
authority and example of vice, and it will require almost a miracle to save it from falling
into the pit of crime.   The inhabitants of a
neighborhood grow to resemble each other in
many ways, owing to the force of mutual suggestion and example.   Removal from one
neighborhood to another—from one town to
another—has changed the life of many persons, for better or for worse.   These facts
should not need further proof or argument—
the use of one's powers of observation should
be sufficient to render them self-evident.

The consideration of the above stated facts
may tend to produce a feeling of sadness or
discouragement in the minds of some who
may read them alone, without reference to the
remedy.   And, indeed it surely would be a
sad and hopeless state of affairs were there
no remedy.   But Nature always supplies an
antidote for every bane—and those who seek
the remedy will always find it.   Nature has

given man a Will—a Will to use and order his
life and character as he will. And by that
Will he is able to *reject and refuse* the suggestions which are not conducive to his welfare
—and to seek, welcome and accept those which
are calculated to strengthen and build up his
character along the desired lines. If man
were but the creature of chance and circumstance, then indeed would he be but as an au-
tomaton moved by the wires of fate, circumstance and environment. But with the possession of the Sovereign Will, he may cast
aside and away from him the injurious things,
and draw to himself those calculated to help
and develop him.

No one is compelled to *accept* a suggestion
—no one is prevented from rejecting one.
On the contrary every person has the power
to choose and decide between the impressions coming to him from the outside world,
and to accept or reject as he wills. By the
proper mental attitude one may cause adverse suggestions to fly from him as the bul-
let is deflected from the steel armor of the
battle-ship. And by turning the attention toward the kind of suggestions he wishes for,

he may discover them and select them as his own from amidst the mass of impressions of the contrary character. One draws his own to him—he finds that for which he seeks. As Kay says: "When one is engaged in seeking for a thing, if he keep the image of it clearly before the mind, he will be very likely to find it, and that too, probably where it would otherwise have escaped his notice. . . . Truly we may say of the mind, as has been said of the eye, that 'it perceives only what it brings with it the power of perceiving." And as John Burroughs has aptly illustrated: "No one ever found the walking fern who did not have the walking fern in his mind. A person whose eye is full of Indian relics, picks them up in every field he walks through. They are quickly recognized because the eye has been commissioned to find them." And the mind may be commissioned to find the things needed and sought for, as well as may be the eye.

Halleck well says, regarding the power of the will to shape one's thoughts, desires and actions, instead of allowing them to be controlled from the outside, along the lines of

Suggestion: "In the capacity for attention, we have the key to the freedom of the will. *Voluntary attention* makes the motive. The motive does not make the attention. Hence the motive is a product of the Will. If I withdraw my attention from a motive idea, it loses vigor, like a plant deprived of air and moisture. . . . By sheer force of will-power, many a one has withdrawn his attention from certain temptations, centered it elsewhere, and thus developed a counter motive." And here is where the individual may make use of the power of outward Suggestion in his own development of character. By refusing to allow his attention to be attracted or held by impressions and suggestions, (or their sources) which are detrimental to his welfare, he renders them ineffective and of no avail. Likewise, by holding his attention ever open for, and then firmly fixed upon those which are conducive to his welfare, he may surround himself with a continuous atmosphere of helpful and uplifting suggestive impressions, which will inspire and strengthen him. Man is the master of Suggestion, if he will but use the Will with which Nature has endowed him.

Under the subject of Auto-Suggestion, which will be considered in the latter part of this book, the reader will find taught a system of self-development, or Character-Building, which will be found not only to develop one along desired lines, but which will also tend to attract to himself suggestive influences in harmony with his own character—for like attracts like in the world of thought and Suggestion, as in every other field of Nature's operations.

CHAPTER VIII.

In the preceding chapter we called your attention to the fact that the period of childhood is one in which mental impressions or suggestions are readily accepted, and firmly retained in the character. This fact is lost sight of by the majority of parents and teachers, who seem to think (if they think of it at all) that the child's mind works precisely like that of the adult. They imagine that a child should be able to *see* and understand the reason of things, and to be amenable to appeals to reason, whereas the child has not fully reached the reasoning stage, as the term is generally used. The child is governed almost altogether by the feelings and emotions, and from the effect of impressions and suggestions received from those around it. This being the case, we may see how careful we should be to avoid the use of improper suggestions to the child; and to use the proper ones. The child naturally accepts the suggestions of its parents, in a way that would surprise the parent could he or she but get a glimpse of the workings of the little mind.

Too often is the child impressed with the idea that "Johnny is such a stubborn child—he cannot be moved when he makes up his mind to a thing." Or, "Edward Everett is *so delicate;* the least thing upsets him. We have to be *so* careful about him." Or "Mary has the *meanest* disposition—she seems to do things just to spite one, and annoy those around her." Or "Samantha is too stupid for anything; she acts as if she wasn't just right in her senses, sometimes." 'And so on, *all in the presence of the child!* 'And the amazing thing is that the parent, or teacher, does not seem to realize that the child listens attentively to what is said, and grows to accept the Suggestion of Authority and Repetition, and naturally acts along the lines of the suggestion. Thought takes form in action, and these mental images manifest themselves in material form. The child feels that he is just what his elders are claiming for him, and naturally falls into line. Long before the parents realize it, the child is forming habits of character from these repeated suggestions made about it in its presence. The process is simple—the child does not *reason* over the matter and then decide to act upon the suggested characteristics. Its subconscious mentality, or habit-mind, simply absorbs these suggested impressions, and when they are repeated many times a day the impression becomes fixed in that region of the mind. Just imagine yourself (*you* who are reading these words) being subjected to a running fire of verbal criticism of this kind. Would you not tend to "make good" the bad qualities attributed to you? Would you not, eventually, grow to play the part assigned to you? That is, if you didn't rebel and change your environment. The child cannot change its environment, but must stay where it is and listen to this perpetual flow of adverse suggestion, week in and week out. And, when you realize that the child's mind is a hundred times more impressionable than is your own, you may begin to understand the effect of these suggestions upon it.

In the same way the repeated remarks of some foolish mothers, that "Eloise is such a beautiful child; people notice her on the streets, and turn around to watch her,"—*this in the presence of the child*—must exert an influence over the mind and future character of that child. And the common suggestion that "Carmencita is *so* bashful; she is always afraid of strangers, and I cannot get her to 'make up' to them"—now, just imagine what that must mean to the sensitive child when she hears it said in her very presence and that of the stranger! How would you feel, if you were sensitive, and your friends should say in your presence when you met a stranger for the first time: "Oh Mr. Brown, you must really excuse Miss Psyche's bashfulness—she is so shy and retiring—she blushes every time she meets a stranger, and cannot think of a word to say!" How would you relish having salt thus rubbed in the open wound of your self-consciousness? Multiply your feelings by ten, and you have the child in question. Cannot you see that you are using the very strongest possible method of developing the self-consciousness of the child—the very means that you would use were you actually *trying to make* the child shy and bashful. Besides the shock to the sensitive nature, you are also actually building character in the child along the lines of the Suggestion of Repetition.

We have seen mothers cry out to children who had picked up an ornament: "Oh, Mabel, you'll *drop* it—look out *it will slip from your fingers*—take it away from her, *quick*, before she *drops* it!"—and more of the same kind. When one realizes that it is by precisely this class of suggestions that suggestible subjects are made to perform actions in experimental psychology, one may wonder why Mabel does not drop the thing at the first suggestion, not to speak of its insistent repetition—and often she does. A kindly, "Put it back in its place, Mabel; mother doesn't like her vases moved about," would be better calculated to preserve the integrity of the vase. Similar to this is the suggestion of: "Oh dear, she'll fall down the stairs—look out dear, *you'll fall; you'll fall in a minute;* look out now!" Can you wonder if the child does fall, after a suggestion like that? Can't you see that you are supplying motive power for the suggested action. In such case, the thing to do is to keep cool, and above everything else not to let the child catch your fearthought. Fear is contagious, by the channel of Suggestion. If you have ever witnessed any experimental work in psychology, in its branch of Suggestion, you may begin to appreciate the motive force latent in a strong Suggestion to an impressionable mind—and children have impressionable minds.

We feel annoyed that we should have to include any reference to the criminal practice of giving children the suggestion of Fright—this subjects belongs to the Dark Ages of child-rearing, but alas! we hear of new instances of its persistence, every few days. When one thinks of the terrors of the little mind due to the suggestions poured into it regarding "Boogy-men"; "Shadow-men"; "Big Bear will Catch You!" "Something will grab your foot if you step out of bed!"; "Better look out when you go up the dark stairs!"; and all the rest of the infernal suggestions of that kind, one feels it difficult to speak with the conventional restraint. We have known women of middle-age who have never been able to outlive these fear-impressions given in early youth. The "Big Bear" is so firmly lodged in their subconscious mind that all their knowledge and reason is not sufficient to eradicate it. As the well-known Englishman, of undoubted bravery and highest reasoning faculties once said: "I laugh at and believe nothing of the grisly things in the daytime; but in the midnight darkness of my bed-chamber I find myself believing in all the horrors of my childish imaginings." And all this the result of these criminal suggestions. Many a child has been rendered "nervous" and "fearful" for the rest of its life, by these "Boogy-boos" of childhood. To one who understands the workings of the Law of Suggestion, such things seem as bad as witchcraft and sorcery.

The reverse of this general proposition is true. Just as adverse suggestions may be harmful to the child, so may the proper ones be helpful. If you must make suggestions to, and about the little one, use as their subjects the favorable points of the child, or those in which you wish the child to improve. In the case of the bashful child, give it the silent Suggestion of Association by ignoring its shyness,

—take no notice of its failing, and see that
your friends act likewise. Soon the child,
seeing that it is not noticed at all, will begin to
evince the natural childish desire to attract attention, and will begin to come out of its shell.
The child with the dirty hands may be put on
its mettle, by calling the attention of friends
to how Johnny is getting to be a big boy now,
and how much cleaner he is keeping his hands
than when he was a little fellow. Always
map your suggestions on *what you want the
children to be,* not what you *fear* they will be,
or are. Just as in Auto-Suggestion, you
hold the mental image of *what you wish to
become,* as a pattern upon which your subconsciousness will model your new character—so
should you ever hold before the child a mental picture of that which you wish it to be. Do
not misunderstand us—we do not mean to
advise *preaching* to the child, no child likes
that—we mean to act, and suggest, that the
child actually *is* becoming or acting as you
wish. You will get the idea better if you will
reverse the line of suggestions objected to by
us in the first part of this chapter. Encourage
the positives—and the negatives will die

away. Cultivate the desirable tendencies, and the undesirable ones will die for want of nourishment.

Above all, realize that the mind of the tiny child is like a soft impression plate, or a sensitive photographic film—therefore be careful what objects of suggestion you place before it. Place bright, strong, positive pictures in its mind, and avoid those of the opposite kind.

In conclusion, we would remind you that the actions, views, ideas, and general life of the parents act as suggestions for the child. "Like Papa and Mama," is the instinctive idea in the mind of every child, from its earliest days. Therefore "Papa and Mama" have considerable responsibility in this direction, during the early days of the child particularly. What Papa or Mama do, is Gospel to the child—everything, good and bad, is worthy of imitation. Suggestion of Imitation is always active in the family. Govern yourselves accordingly. Teachers have the same responsibility—"Teacher does it," is a sufficient excuse for the child. There is always a case of "a chiel' among us, takin' notes."

And these notes are suggestive notes. We feel that a whole book might well be written on this subject, in order to do it even faint justice. But we trust that the hints that we have given here may reach some for whom they are intended, and who need them very much. You may not be able to give your children the riches or "advantages" that you would like to bestow upon them (perhaps that is so much the better for them) but you have the opportunity of giving them the best possible Suggestions—the "best in the shop," and that is *much*, very much indeed.

PART II

THERAPEUTIC SUGGESTION

CHAPTER IX.

Perhaps in no other way is Suggestion so commonly accepted by people as in relation to their physical condition, or health. People are being made sick, and others are being made well, every day by Suggestion pure and simple. We purpose devoting a number of the chapters of this book to various phases of Suggestive Therapeutics, but it may be as well, at this point, to call your attention to the undoubted effect of Suggestion upon the physiological functions. Science has recognized this fact, and modern medicine takes it into serious consideration. Cults and schools of thought have been built upon this fact, and the underlying principle has been lost sight of by the various theories, explanations, dogmas and ideas philosophical and theological which have gathered around it. Some of the authorities call it "The Effect of the Imagination upon Physical States," or "The Power of Mind over Body"—but Suggestion is the active principle of application in all the various forms, and under all the various names, and in spite of the conflicting theories.

That mental states affect physiological function is admitted by the best authorities in medical science, and has been for many years. But it is only of later years that methods of applying the principle have been taught and practiced to any great extent. Previous to that time the principle was mentioned only in connection with the production or induction of disease by adverse mental states. Perhaps a consideration of the older authorities might be interesting and instructive, at this stage, and before we undertake the general subject of Suggestive Therapeutics.

Sir Samuel Baker, in the *British and Foreign Medico-Chirurgical Review*, said: "Any severe grief or anger is almost certain to be succeeded by fever, in certain parts of Africa." Sir B. W. Richardson, said: "Diabetes from sudden mental shock is a true, pure type of a physical malady of mental origin." Sir George Paget, said: "In many cases I have seen reasons for believing that cancer has had its origin in prolonged anxiety." Dr. Murchison said: "I have been surprised how often patients with primary cancer of the liver have traced the cause of this ill-health to protracted grief or anxiety. The cases have been far too numerous to be accounted for as mere coincidences." Prof. Elmer Gates, says: "My experiments show that irascible, malevolent and depressing emotions generate in the system injurious compounds, some of which are extremely poisonous; also that agreeable, happy emotions generate chemical compounds of nutritious value, which stimulate the cells to manufacture energy." Dr. F. W. Southworth says: "If mental causes can change the various secretions of the body, making them poisonous, for example, the saliva, and the milk in the human breast, under the influence of anger, worry or fear, could it not also be productive of disease through imperfect or non-elimination? Is it improbable that fear, which is a greater negative force than anger, may produce the results as indicated?" All of the mental states above-mentioned as affording a probable cause of disease can be and are produced by Suggestion or Auto-Sugges-

tion. While that mysterious force behind
the mental states may escape our definition,
unless we consider it to be some phase of the
Will, nevertheless we may safely assert that
in Suggestion we find the motive power which
calls this force into operation.

In the same way, that which people call
"Imagination," is seen to be but a mental
picture created in the imaginative regions of
the mind by Suggestion, and afterward mate-
rialized by Fear or Faith, both of which act
in the same general manner. The following
interesting quotation from Prof. Halleck will
show the effect of these suggested mental
images, considered as products of the Imagination: "When a mental image is taken for a
reality, the most astonishing results often follow; indeed, sometimes they are more pro-
nounced than if the image were a reality. One
may find many illustrations of this in every-
day life. . . . Were it not for this
power of the imagination, the majority of
quack nostrums would disappear. In most
cases bread pills, properly labeled, with positive assurances of certain cure accompanying
them, would answer the purpose far better

than these nostrums, or even much better than a great deal of the medicine administered by regular physicians. . . . There is perhaps not a person living who would not at times be benefited by a bread pill, administered by some one in whom great confidence was reposed. . . . Warts have been charmed away by medicines which could have had only a mental effect. Dr. Tuke gives many cases of patients cured of rheumatism by rubbing them with a certain substance declared to possess magic power. The material in some cases was metal; in others wood; in still others, wax. He also recites the case of a very intelligent officer who had vainly taken powerful remedies to cure cramp in the stomach. Then he was told that on the next attack he would be put under a medicine which was generally believed to be most effective, but which was rarely used. When the cramps came on again, a powder containing four grains of ground biscuit was administered every seven minutes, while the greatest anxiety was expressed (within the hearing of the party) lest too much should be given. Half-drachm doses of bismuth had never procured the same relief in less than three hours. For four successive times did the same kind of attack recur, and four times was it met by the same remedy, and with like success. A house surgeon in a French hospital experimented with one hundred patients, giving them sugared water. Then, with a great show of fear, he pretended that he had made a mistake and given them an emetic instead of the proper medicine. Dr. Tuke, says of this case: 'The result may easily be anticipated by those who can estimate the influence of the imagination. No fewer than eighty—four-fifths—were unmistakably sick.' "

You are familiar with the old cases of people who have been told repeatedly that they were looking very sick, as a practical joke, and who took to their beds with various ailments. Also of the man who thought he was bleeding to death, from hearing the dripping of water accompanying a slight incision made in his arm by surgeons—actual death ensuing from the shock and fright. Many similar cases are related in the annals of medicine. Every professor in a medical college has had numerous experiences in which students took on the symptoms of the various diseases which they had been studying. It has been estimated that as many die from fright during great epidemics, as from the disease itself. We have had the personal assurance of a reputable practitioner of medicine, that he once attended a case in which the patient believed that she had taken a dose of strychnine by mistake. When the physician arrived the patient was showing all the symptoms of poisoning from strychnine (she had previously witnessed the death of a dog from a similar poison) and only recovered after the usual antidotes and treatments had been administered—as it was she was weak for a long time afterward, notwithstanding the fact that after the doctor had left, the bottle of poison was found untouched, the woman having taken some harmless mixture. Many physicians of long practice relate similar experiences in their own professional life. Fright is a virulent poison, in many cases— just as joy is a powerful restorative and invigorant.

Dr. Geo. R. Patton in a paper read before a medical society in 1900, made the following statements: "The mind as a dynamic force exerted over the functions of the body has been, doubtless, operatively manifest from the cradle of our existence. Though the fact may not have been so recognized at this primitive period, it is really the explanation of the cures which were then attributed to the influence of the stars, to divinations, talismans, charms, *et id omne genus;* for in the infancy of our race there were neither doctors nor drugs, the means of cure being wholly mental, aided by the so-called 'efforts of nature.' Herodotus tells us that the Babylonians, Chaldeans, and other nations of antiquity had no other physicians and used no medicines. Even when the practice of healing passed from the East into Egypt, and thence into Greece, it was exclusively confined to the temples. At this period it was the universal belief that all diseases were due to the anger of the gods, and, therefore, prayers, with ceremonies of pomp and mysticism were used to propitiate heaven in favor of the sick, and all were of such a nature as to act vividly upon the imagination and emotions. . . . Now these measures, in their entirety, were well calculated to arouse a new and favoring action in the nervous centres, and through them a sanative influence over the assimilative and nutritive processes, as well as upon the organic functions. At a later period, when medicine first began to be disseminated from Greece into the outer world . . . if recovery took place it was accredited wholly to a charm, incantation, amulet or talisman, which had now, in part, taken the place of the ceremonies in the temple, as the means of cure. Here, again, we see the effects of credulity and superstition exercised through the emotions and imagination upon the ills of the body. At still a later period in the history of medicine, magic and medicine were almost synonymous terms; in fact, the practice of medicine consisted almost wholly of the machinery of magic. A word scrawled upon parchment, for instance, would cure fevers; a hexameter from the Iliad of Homer cured gout, while rheumatism succumbed to a verse from Lamentations. These could be multiplied, and undoubtedly all were equally potent of cure in like manner. The repulsive and ridiculous agents at one time so often and so freely given to the sick could only have been curative through a mental impression transmitted to the body; for who could take a potion from the skull of a murderer; or a tincture made from the common louse; or a pill from the dried liver of a bat; or a powder from the heads and legs of spiders, without profound emotion? Even now, new, unusual and untried remedies are often more efficient than the old and well-tried ones, and the shrewd and knowing doctor often avails himself of this fact.''

In each and every one of the instances mentioned above the effect was undoubtedly caused by the power of Suggestion, in one or more of its various forms and phases. We shall continue this subject in the next chapter.

CHAPTER X.

Not only in the ancient days was Suggestion, under various disguises employed to arouse the minds of the people in such a manner that therapeutic benefits were secured, but even in comparatively recent history—yes, even down to the present times, have the same general methods been employed with the same results. History constantly repeats itself, in Suggestive Therapeutics as in everything else.

All through the history of the race for the past thousand years, we find numerous instances of the employment of "Masked Suggestion"—that is Suggestion wearing the veil of some outward form or belief—operating to cure people of disease. We hear countless instances of holy wells, sacred grottoes, sacred relics, shrines, and other places associated with various religions, to which have been attributed wonderful cures of physical ailments. Many supposedly incurable cases have been healed at these places, or by these holy objects. The shrines, and wells, and chapels are filled with the crutches of cured cripples, and countless well attested cases of marvelous cures are reported as having occurred. But similar cures have been recorded throughout all history, accompanying all forms of religions, so that the scientific investigator soon comes to the conclusion that the only virtue in the religious association of the cure consists in the faith and association in the mind of the patient, along the lines of Suggestion. The same results are obtained by so many different methods, and under so many different phases of religious belief, both Christian and "pagan," that it must be conceded that the real cause lies far back of creed, form, or ceremonial. And Suggestion is seen to be the real cause. There is a well-known case related of a "Sacred Bone" which obtained great repute in the Middle-Ages from its wonderful power to heal diseases. This bone had been brought from the Holy Land by two soldiers of the crusades, and was supposed to be a portion of the skeleton of some great character of the New Testament. It was only upon the death of one of these soldiers, years after, that the truth became known. On his death-bed the soldier confessed that he and his companion becoming drunk on the journey, had lost the real relic which they were transporting from the Holy Land. Fearing to return home without it, they substituted the bone of a sheep which they found in a field. Much to their surprise this sheep-bone operated as the means of wonderful cures, and they agreed to keep the matter silent. In this case, as in many other of a similar nature, the faith and belief of the people, acting along the lines of Suggestion, operated as a dynamic power for producing physiological changes and operations, which resulted in the restoration of health to many a suffering mortal. After the disclosure of the nature of the relic, the cures ceased at once, and many of those who had been healed became sick again.

The kings of England and France were formerly believed to possess great healing powers, applied by laying on the hands. This was known as the "Royal Touch" and was believed to be specially efficacious in cases of scrofula. Thousands were cured of this and similar diseases, and the gift was never doubted. Wiseman, a noted surgeon of several centuries past, has written of the Royal Touch: "I myself have been an eye-witness of many thousands of cures performed by his majesty's touch alone, without the assistance of medicine or surgery, and those, many of them, such as had tired out the endeavors of able surgeons before they came hither. I must needs profess that what I write will little more than show the weakness of our ability when compared with his majesty's, who cureth more in one year than all the surgeons of London have done in an age." The virtue of the Royal Touch was not doubted, until in the seventeenth century when there arose a pretender by the name of Greatrakes, who claimed to possess the Royal Touch, and who healed thousands of people by laying on of hands. So marked was his influence that the throne became worried, for the people were muttering that Greatrakes must be the descendant of a former king, and rightful heir to the throne. The Royal Chirurgical Society of London investigated Greatrakes and his cures, and made a report stating that his cures arose from "some mysterious sanative contagion in his body." Modern students of Suggestion give a more scientific explanation.

Similar to these cases is that of Elijah Perkins, a Connecticut blacksmith, who invented a set of "metallic tractors," which were a tong-shaped contrivance composed of several kinds of metal. These tractors were applied to the affected portions of the body, and wonderful cures were reported as the result. A great furor arose from the character and number of cures thus made by Perkins, and he founded a school of the healing art which was called "Perkinism." New England was set ablaze by the new wonder, and the contagion rapidly spread over the rest of the country. Thence it was carried to England and the Continent, with equal success. Schools and hospitals were erected, in which "Perkinism" was practiced. The records of the time state that over a million cures were made in Europe alone. People high and low, were treated with more or less success. The bubble was finally punctured by Dr. Haygarth of London, who held that the cures resulted from the imagination rather than from any virtue inherent in the tractors. Accordingly he proceeded to prove this theory, in the following manner, as reported by a chronicler of the time: "He formed pieces of wood into the shape of tractors, and with much assumed pomp and ceremony applied them to a number of sick persons who had been previously prepared to expect something extraordinary. The effects were found to be astonishing. Obstinate pains in the limbs were suddenly cured; joints that had long been immovable were restored to motion, and, in short, except the renewal of lost parts or the change in mechanical structure, nothing seemed beyond their power to accomplish." These results, when explained, punctured the bubble of "Perkinism," and the craze subsided. In this case, as in the other the "imagination" was simply a form of Suggestion along the lines of which we have spoken in preceding chapters.

The success of Dowieism, and similar religious or semi-religious cults all go to prove the same thing—the existence of some fundamental principle underlying all of these opposing claims, which operates whenever and

however it may be invoked. Dowie undoubtedly cured thousands of people in spite of the
crudeness of his methods and creed, and in
spite of the ridiculous nature of his claims.
And so it is and has been, and will be with other
similar cults. They make about the same
percentage of cures, because they apply the
same fundamental principle of Suggestion
masked by their various creeds, beliefs and
forms of application. The Emmanuel Movement which is attracting so much attention at
this time, employs the same fundamental principle, but unlike its predecessors it frankly
acknowledges the nature of that principle, and
admits that it is Suggestion. The religious
atmosphere and influence surrounding these
"church-cures" is especially adapted to
arousing the feelings of faith, belief and religious emotion in the patient, and these are
among the strongest emotive factors in mental
cures, as they serve to bring into operation the
dynamic force of the mind of the patient,
which tends to restore normal functioning. In
fact, we freely admit that many of these cures
would not have been accomplished by the
methods of the ordinary practitioner of Sug-

gestion, for the reason that the latter would not have been able to arouse the emotional power of the patient sufficiently. The greater amount of emotive power and expectant attention that the healer is able to arouse in the patient, the better are the chances of a cure.

Physicians know the value of the "placebo," which is simply a harmless prescription, consisting either of flavored water, or a pill of no medicinal effect, or similar thing. It is the idea of the celebrated "bread-pill." Every physician knows of many marvelous cures effected by these harmless "medicines," the effect depending altogether upon what the physicians formerly called "imagination," but which they now know as Suggestion. Sir Humphrey Davy once cured a difficult case, by the virtue of the clinical thermometer, which the patient declared made him feel much better the moment it was applied to his mouth. Many patent-medicine cures have been made in the same way. The various decoctions formerly sold by the street-corner fakirs in the country towns, cured people in the same way. The thousand-and-one appliances and contrivances so extensively adver-

tised in the rural newspapers, depend upon
Suggestion for their curative virtue. They
all make cures—and in the same way.

Now all this does not mean simply that
these "imaginary" cures are unreal, or cures
of imaginary diseases, as so many have assumed. It simply means that they act in the
direction of arousing the dynamic latent
forces of the mind, along the lines of Suggestion. And these mental forces are sufficiently
powerful to act and react upon the bodily functions and organs. None of us need to be told
of the fact that mental states have a direct effect upon physical functions. Who does not
know the effect of fear, grief, or joy on the
functions of digestion, assimilation and elimination? The change of a mental state reacts
upon the physical system at once. We lose
appetite upon the receipt of bad news; but
good news makes us feel like enjoying the
meal. A disgusting sight, or recollection will
produce nausea. The thought of certain
food will cause the saliva to flow, and the gastric juices to be secreted. There is no nonsense, or fanciful imagination about these
things—they are psycho-physiological facts,

known and taught in text-books upon the subject.

And sane, rational, scientific Suggestive Therapeutics is based upon this fundamental principle of action and re-action between mind and body, or rather between the brainmind and the mind in the cells and organs of the body, for it is now known that there is mind in every cell and centre of the physical body. In the chapters following the present one, we shall call your attention to both the theory and practice of Suggestive Therapeutics, as taught by the best authorities of today. It is a subject well worth the careful attention and study of every thinking person.

CHAPTER XI.

The term, "Suggestive Therapeutics" has sprung into popular use during the past ten years, by reason of the fact that Suggestion has come to be recognized in regular medical circles as a valuable method of treating many forms of mental and physical disorders. While the term is often used in its narrow significance of treatment by Suggestion as Suggestion, with the full knowledge on the part of the patient of the underlying principle, still it is properly applicable in all cases of healing or treatment of disease in which the mental activities are brought to bear on the body, by means of masked suggestions, advice, or "statements" of the various schools of metaphysical healing, including the religious or quasi-religious sects and cults. In this broad sense, Suggestive Therapeutics today must be recognized as one of the most popular and commonly used methods of treatment of physical disorders. And, brushing aside the fanatical claims and theories of some of the cults, there will be found a solid foundation of fact underlying the various methods employed.

Suggestive Therapeutics as a science is emerging from the mists and clouds of superstition and fanatical statements and beliefs, and is asserting its right to be considered as any other science—on its merits, and with a fair and open mind. This is being recognized by many of the leading minds in and out of the medical profession, although many of the ultra-conservatives still linger in the rear, protesting against the innovation. But constant progress is being made. As Max Eastman says in a recent magazine article: "The mission of this paper is to offer guidance in a matter about which a great quantity of the general public is very much at sea. In this question of 'mind over matter,' the reformers have done their work. They have stirred things up. They have bestowed upon the world about a hundred and fifty little religions and a confused idea that there must be some truth in the matter somewhere. The ignorant have done their work. They have perse-

cuted the believers, jeered at them, or damned
them with a vacuous smile. This world will
never lack ballast. It is only the scientists
that have failed of their duty. They have
stalked through a routine of elevated lectures,
written a few incomprehensible books, and
kept the science of Psychology, so far as the
hungry world goes, sealed up in their own
proud bosoms. In all this uproar of faith-
cures, and miracles, and shouting prophets, we
have heard few illuminating words from the
universities. The consequence is that we are
without a helm, and the reform blows now one
way and now another.''

The rapid rise of what is known as "The
Emmanuel Movement" has served to bring a
great number of conservative people to realize
that many cures may be made by Suggestive
Therapeutics, pure and simple, under the aus-
pices of church organizations, but without the
accessories of fanciful metaphysical beliefs or
theories. The fact that these Emmanuel healers are accomplishing the same results, without making the claims of metaphysical schools
on the one hand, or the claims of a monopoly
of the healing power on the other, has opened

the eyes of many people who heretofore have thought that the healing power of the cults was due to some special power not connected with the ordinary natural principles recognized by science. The Emmanuel Movement is yet in its infancy, and there is room for great improvement in some of its methods, but the honesty of its teachers and healers cannot be questioned, and there has been manifested a steadfast determination to avoid claiming any miraculous powers or monopoly of truth. The rise and popularity of this movement is a hopeful sign, and one that encourages those outside of the movement who have long been interested in the subject of Suggestive Therapeutics.

At the same time there is to be found, both in this country and abroad, a rapidly growing body of earnest workers among the ranks of the medical profession, who use Suggestion in their practice, with excellent results. These men have found that many disorders which were formerly considered as having purely physical causes, really have their roots and causes in mental states and conditions. Consequently they treat the source of the trouble, instead of the symptoms, with excellent results. And, these men have also found that even in cases of purely physical troubles, the mind may be directed toward strengthening and stimulating the various organs to normal functioning, by means of Suggestion. And it is here that the great field for future investigation and experiment opens out to these earnest seekers after truth in their profession. The day for antagonism between the "Mind-Cure" people outside of the medical profession, and the practitioners of "Suggestive Therapeutics" within the profession, has past. The era of mutual understanding and co-operation has arrived. We are speaking now of the people, on both sides, who have truth and results as their sole object and aim —but where personal gain is allowed to interfere, there must always be jealousies and friction.

In order to give you a fair idea of the general opinion of the medical practitioners of "Suggestive Therapeutics," we ask that you read the following quotation from Max Eastman's magazine article, before referred to. Dr. Eastman says: "The Law of Suggestion, which is one of the great discoveries of modern science, was first formulated by Dr. Liebault at Paris, in a book published in 1866. Since his day the number of physicians who practice 'suggestive therapeutics' has steadily increased, until to-day no thorough clinical hospital is without a professional suggestionist. The practice does not involve any metaphysical theories, the passage of any hidden force from one brain to another, any 'planes of existence,' or any religious upset, or any poetic physiology, or the swallowing of any occult doctrines whatever. It is one of the simplest and coolest of scientific theories. It is a question of the relation between the brain and the bodily organs. It seems never to have been clearly stated that healing disease by suggestion depends not in the least degree upon any theory of the relation of mind and matter. . . . The attempt to fix an idea in the mind without reason is suggestion. It is accomplished usually in medical practice by asking the patient to lie down and relax his body and his mind and then vigorously stating to him the desired idea. It may be accomplished in a number of ways. The patient may be told that the operator is a wizard and is about to transfer an idea from his own mind to that of the patient. If the patient believes him he will very likely accept the idea. It may be accomplished by gestures or incantations which the patient regards with superstitious awe, provided it is explained beforehand what these gestures are meant to produce. It may be accomplished by telling the patient he has no body, and sitting with him for a while in spiritual silence, provided he knows what to expect. All these methods, if one believes in them, are good, and they prove by their success the law of suggestion. But the method that is based on a sure truth is the method of the scientist. He reasons with his patient, he stirs in him what moral and religious enthusiasm he can, and to these means he adds tactfully the subtle suggestive powers of his own presence and eloquence. This force, together with the power which is revealed in a man of correcting his own mental habits, is the greatest practical discovery of modern psychology. . . . Suggestive therapeutics is the use of suggestion to fix in the mind ideas of health, or healthy mental habits.''

Dr. Eastman has well expressed the scientific view of Suggestive Therapeutics in the above quotation. He calls attention to the fact that while scientific suggestionists recognize the fact that in a number of persons the fanciful appeals to superstition, credulity, and fantastic theories will yield beneficial results, still the tendency and desire is toward educating the patient up to an intelligent understanding of the nature of the principle of cure, and the actual operations thereof. This, of course, should be the aim of every true suggestionist, although personally we can understand the position of some practitioners whose patients are largely recruited from among the ignorant classes, and who would simply mystify and bewilder their patients were they to attempt to explain the scientific principles of Suggestion. These practitioners may be excused when they claim that "the end justifies the means," and in their position that in the case of the very ignorant patient the best way is to *cure him first,* and then to explain so far as is possible, afterward. In this spirit there are many physicians who, recognizing a case for Suggestive treatment in a patient of this class, consider that the best way to administer that suggestion is by means of colored, flavored and sweetened water, or other *placebo,* accompanied by strong, positive repeated suggestions of *what the medicine will do for the patient.* A *placebo* administered in this way, a half-teaspoonful to be taken every half-hour, becomes a most powerful suggestion. In the first place, there is the strong Suggestion of Authority of the physician, and the Suggestion of Repetition which is caused by the frequent taking of the dose, each dose being a reminder of the original Suggestion. Many cases reached in this way, could not be reached by ordinary Suggestion, with a scientific explanation—the patient wouldn't understand it at all. In the same way a little trip, or a visit to some celebrated springs or health resort, acts as a strong suggestion, as all physicians know. These things all have their place, and have their uses and excuses; but the practitioner does not complete his work unless he finally dismisses the patient with a number of good suggestions, and a stock of good advice regarding personal habits, etc., which will tend to prevent a recurrence of the complaint.

No work, or chapters, on Suggestive Therapeutics would be complete without a consideration of the causes of the physical complaints amenable to the suggestive treatment. Therefore in the succeeding chapter we shall consider the same. In this part of the work we shall draw upon the knowledge and experience of some able practitioners, in and out of the medical profession, with whom we have been associated in experimental psychological work, in addition to actual cases which have come under our own personal experience. We shall avoid technical terms so far as is possible, as this book is in no sense of the term to be considered a "medical work."

CHAPTER XII.

In order to understand the principles underlying Suggestive Therapeutics, we must consider the physiological causes of disease, or at least the first manifest physiological stage of disease. The best authorities now hold that disease is caused primarily by the failure of the cells to do their duty, or to repair their waste. Of course, it may be urged that there are mental causes behind this manifestation which operate in the direction of interfering with the activities or vigor of the cells. This we are prepared to admit, but even so it must be granted that in the above failure to function properly the cells manifest the first physiological stage of disease. This trouble may arise from the inefficiency or rebellion of a single cell, which then spreads its contagion to those around it, or else to a rebellion on the part of a group of cells. Or from a failure of various groups of cells to coordinate and co-operate. There are certain

actions among cell-groups which so closely resemble a mutiny, or rebellion, that it is impossible to avoid using the figurative term in
describing them.

Each individual cell is a tiny life, having its
various functions and activities—its mental
as well as its physical side. Cells show varying degrees of what may well be called "intelligence." They have their memories, and
profit by experience. They co-operate with
other cells and often seemingly have civil war
among themselves. Any failure on the part
of the cells, or cell-groups to do their work,
results in the symptoms which we call
"disease." According to the size and loca-
tion of the cell-disturbance does the disease
become local or general. The disease is cured,
either when the rebellious cells are forced to
resume normal functioning, or else when they
have been discarded and destroyed and replaced by new healthy normal cells which perform the tasks which their predecessors have
abandoned. Therefore, any method or means
which operates in the direction of restoring
normal function to the cells, in the direction
of stimulating, regulating, or removing obsta-

cles, tends to produce what it called a cure.
And to this end Nature is constantly directing
her efforts. And Nature is helped by the
proper mental attitudes, or retarded by improper ones. Faith and confident expectation are wonderful aids to Nature in this work,
while Fear and Apprehension are obstacles
and detriments.

Recent discoveries have confirmed the views
of the thinkers of a few years back who identi-
fied the mind in the cells, with a portion of
that wonderful region of the mind called the
subconscious. Each cell has mind in it, and
belonging to it, but the various "minds" of
the cells have mental filaments connecting with
each other, and all connecting with the entire
subconscious region of the mind. Therefore
anything affecting the subconscious mind must
of necessity affect the cells themselves, in
varying degrees. Through the subconscious
mind, and the sympathetic nervous system,
are worked many important physiological
changes. The concentration of attention upon
any part of the body is known to affect the
circulation of that part, and every student of
Suggestive Therapeutics is aware that the

concentration of the patients thought upon any organ coupled with the idea of that organ being diseased is very apt to be followed by symptoms of imperfect functioning in the organ in question. Likewise the concentration of the attention upon an organ or part, with the idea that the organ has been invigorated and stimulated to proper and normal functioning, is very apt to be followed by results in accordance with the idea. To endeavor to explain "just why" this is so, would take us into the realm of theory, in which our own views would probably conflict with those of other thinkers upon the subject. More important than any theories are the known facts in the case—the facts stated above.

Physiologists interested in Suggestive Therapeutics endeavor to take the subject away from the region of Mental Science, and seek of find the explanation in the direction of the circulation by the attention, thereby building up the affected parts. Some speak, also of the increased flow of nervous energy to the affected part, by reason of the concentrated attention, and the expectancy. Along these lines, Dr. Eastman says: "Our question is:

Can those physical conditions of the brain affect the physical condition of the stomach? We know that the brain-condition which accompanies the idea of the raising our hand can affect the condition of the muscles of our arm—and we call that a voluntary function. Now the question is whether the brain condition which accompanies the idea of enlivening our stomach can have any effect upon that involuntary function. Experiments with suggestion have proved that in some cases it can, if it continues long enough. Persons of a very suggestible nature, can, for instance, by concentrating their mind upon a certain part of the body, increase the flow of blood to that part, although the regulation of blood flow is supposed to be entirely involuntary. The action of the heart, also the movements of the digestive organs particularly, and of the organs of elimination, are almost directly affected in suggestible persons by that change in their brains which accompanies certain ideas. . . . Science has established, then, that suggestion can effect to some extent, the so-called involuntary functions of the body; but the extent or limitation of these effects is by no means determined. It could not be determined scientifically without years of diligent experiment and tabulation. Any dogmatic statement upon one side or the other of that question is therefore premature and against the spirit of science.''

Along these same general lines, many writers on Suggestive Therapeutics have proceeded from the fundamental position that the healing effects result from the increased circulation and nerve-currents, directed to the affected parts by the unconscious volition of the patient which is aroused and directed by means of the suggestions given him. In this way the weakened digestive apparatus receives an additional amount of nervous force, and an increased circulation, both of which, as all physiologists admit, will tend to stimulate and invigorate the particular part, and be conducive to a resumption of normal functioning. That the circulation may be so directed is unquestioned. It is an axiom of Suggestive Therapeutics that: ''The Circulation follows the Attention,'' and increased circulation means increased nourishment and building material. If the increased circulation be accompanied by increased stimulation by nerve currents, then it must be seen that an improved condition of the part or organ must result. Whether we accept this explanation as the last word in Suggestive Therapeutics, or whether we regard it as merely the statement of effects resulting from higher causes, we must admit that the circulation may be directed by the attention, and that stimulation must result from the increased circulation. The experiments of the psychological laboratories have shown us conclusively that the circulation may be increased in a hand or foot by simple suggestion. Personally, we have conducted experiments in which by suggestion the blood was increased in one hand and decreased in the other, at the same time—one hand assuming a dark red color, while the other appeared pallid. This result, of course, arose from the unconscious volition of the patient, directed by the suggestions given and accepted by him. Results far more startling are common to all experimenters along these lines. This being so, we can see the strength of the argument of those who claim that by this increased circulation in the affected part, accompanied by an increased stimulation by nerve currents directed in the same way, and at the same time, the cures of Suggestive Therapeutics may be explained.

Personally, we think that the above theory or explanation is merely a half-truth. While freely admitting that increased circulation and nerve force is present in the cure, we think that there is still more to the process. Realizing the presence of mind in every cell, cell-group, and part of the body, we think that these "cell-minds" are acted upon by the central mind, just as the subconscious central mind is acted upon by the suggestions from outside. In other words, we believe that the central mind *superimposes* upon the "cell-minds" the suggestions given and accepted by it and thus produces activities in accordance therewith. To use a clumsy illustration let us suppose a still body of water in which the sun is shining—there is but *one* reflection of the sun. Let something stir the body of water so that a portion of it is sprayed into the air as a thousand drops, and in each drop we find the reflection duplicated. In the same way the one suggestion accepted by the subconscious mind is apparently multiplied and reproduced in each cell of the body. In this way we believe that there is a direct mental influence upon the cells, independent of the benefit of the increased circulation and nerve currents. In fact, it may be possible that the increased circulation and nerve force is directed toward the part *because the cells demand it* by reason of the activity aroused within them.

In some forms of mental treatment there appears to be a "short-circuit" established directly between the mind of the suggestor, and the minds in the cells. In such cases the suggestions are directed to the affected parts, in a peculiar manner which shall be described in a later chapter. Some claim that this is but a masked form of plain suggestion, but we have seen results obtained by this method which seemed to render possible, or probable, the existence of some direct connection or "short-circuit," such as we have described. We shall not argue this point, for theories make but little difference in the practical work. We shall now proceed to a consideration of the several best methods for applying Suggestive Therapeutics. By applying these methods you will be able to secure results from which you may deduce your own theories, or adopt those which seem to best fit the facts of the case. Long experience has caused us to regard any and all theories as but working hypotheses, to be applied in action. The final theory is probably still a long way off.

CHAPTER XIII.

The methods of application of Suggestive Therapeutics are as numerous as the many practitioners, for nearly every practitioner employs a method or methods of his own, based upon what he has learned and modified by his own experience. Each practitioner has some favorite method which is generally a modification of that of his teacher or teachers, the modification being determined by the result of his own experience, his temperament, his general philosophy of cure, and his previous training. But the underlying principle is the same. The practitioner who has received the regular medical training is very apt to mould his suggestions along the lines of his previous practice, with a tendency toward *placebos* or harmless preparations with which the suggestions are mingled. The giving of a number of small pellets accompanied with the suggestion that they will produce certain effects is a very effective form of Suggestion, particularly if the patient has been accustomed to drugs and inoculated with a belief in the wonderful potencies of strange decoctions. In the same way a flavored fluid, taken at intervals of a half-hour, with the suggestion that certain results will follow, is a strong medium of Suggestion. Some practitioners give electrical treatments accompanied with strong Suggestions that certain physical changes will occur—and they get results. Others employ manipulations, rubbings, and similar methods, accompanied with strong Suggestion. In fact the suggestive accompaniment may be, and is, employed to advantage in almost every form of treatment. The knowledge of the potency of Suggestion gives the physician the key to the effect of many remedies which some physicians use with excellent results, while others find valueless. A drug, *plus Suggestion,* is an entirely different thing from the same drug, *minus Suggestion.* It is very difficult to determine the exact therapeutic value of any remedy, unless the element of Suggestion in its application be carefully weighed and considered.

If the practitioner happens to belong to any

of the various metaphysical or "New Thought" cults or schools, he will naturally model his suggestions along the lines of his belief. He will urge upon the patient certain teachings of his school, and if the patient be impressed by his earnestness and belief an excellent therapeutic effect is obtained. This idea, however, is vigorously opposed by many of the metaphysical practitioners, who hold that the healing is accomplished by reason of the virtue of their various dogmas, beliefs, and formulas—the proof of the same being apparently established by the number of cures obtained by them. "Our beliefs, dogmas, or theories *must* be so," they say, "else how could we obtain these wonderful cures?" This would be all very well, were it not for the fact that some other healer, with dogmas diametrically opposed to those of the first one, obtains cures of precisely the same nature, and in about the same percentage. The unprejudiced investigator is compelled to believe that the cures result, not from any special virtue residing in the several forms of metaphysical belief or theory, but simply because the patient's faith and expectant attention is aroused by the practitioner, and an unconscious arousing and directing of his own mental energy is obtained by reason thereof.

Anything that serves to inspire confidence and faith in the patient, also serves to turn his mental forces to the affected part in the direction of a stimulating influence and corresponding improvement. The healing force is inherent in the mind of the patient himself,—all the healer can do is to direct it to advantage. Some forms of metaphysical healing are better adapted to certain patients than are others; but other patients must seek other forms best adapted to their temperament, prejudices and training. This fact is known to, and accepted by advanced students of scientific Suggestion, although disputed by the advocates of the many schools and cults. It is a very simple thing when it is considered in the light of reason. Schools A, B and C, have dogmas, doctrines and formulas diametrically opposed to each other. If one be right, the others must be wrong. And if the healing is dependent upon the virtues of the belief, theory or formulas, then it would follow that none but the *true* school could obtain results.

But what are the facts of the case? It is admitted by all scientific investigators, *that all of the three* will obtain the same kind of cures, in the same percentages, providing the practitioners are equally adapted for the work, and suited to the temperament of the patients.

No one who has ever studied the subject will deny that Dowie obtained many wonderful cures—but who would think of ascribing them to any special virtue in his methods or dogmas? Outside of his band of followers his claims are seen to be ridiculous. *Yet he made his cures.* Why? Because he obtained a Suggestive effect by reason of the belief, confidence, and expectant attention he aroused in his followers. Students of Suggestion who attended many of Dowie's healing meetings saw the most active employment of Suggestion in every process of the healing. Of course Dowie denied this, and abused those who so held. He claimed that he was inspired by God, and that God did the healing through him—Suggestion, he held, was the work of the Devil, and was but an imitation of the true method, just as the Egyptian magicians produced snakes in imitation of those produced by

Moses. He claimed that just as Moses' snake swallowed the others, so would Zion swallow the imitators. But it didn't!

In the same way the various leaders, teachers, and practitioners of the various cults, each claim that their way is the Truth, and that all others are base imitations. They are often forced to admit the cures of the rival healers, but they have the habit of saying: "Oh, well, they may *seem* to cure; but their cures won't last—ours alone will be permanent;" or: "others may *cure*, but we alone *heal*." In short, they claim to have the only real article—all the others are imitators. They are like the Bowery second-hand clothes dealer, who put up the sign: "don't go to my imitators to be cheated—*come to me!*" But gradually the public is beginning to awaken to the truth that the real healing power resides within the patient himself, and that *any* method that serves to arouse that inherent power will tend toward the cure. *The method that is capable of arousing that power to the greatest degree, is the best method for that particular patient.* When this fact is recognized, it will be seen that each and every school and cult has its particular place, and reaches certain people as no other form could do. The recognition of this fact should disarm the conflicting factions and cults, and cause them to see good in each other. There is need for a greater tolerance, broadness and charity in the various cults.

To give you an idea of how some of the metaphysical cults employ masked Suggestion in their healing work, we shall quote several of their "treatments." The student, who has grasped the underlying principle, should have no trouble in discovering the seed of Suggestion in these "treatments." These "treatments" are but the capsule, or sugar-coated pellet, in which the remedy is concealed. But remember this, always, that many people need the capsule, and the sugar-coating—they would refuse to accept *straight*, undisguised, and undiluted Suggestion if it were offered to them.

The following treatment for *nervousness*, is followed by a certain cult: "I am *warmed* and fed and clothed and *healed*, by Divine Love." This the patient is instructed to "repeat over and over" many times during the day. Surely it is calculated to produce a restful and peaceful feeling in one of a strong religious temperament. Another "treatment" for Sore Feet, used by the same cult is as follows: "My feet can never be weary nor sore. God created my feet perfect. I walk the pathway of life in perfect ease and comfort. All the obstacles in my path have vanished, and my feet are bathed in a sea of pure love." The patient with the sore feet is instructed to "Mentally place yourself in an attitude to realize the power of the words you utter, for the fulness of peace and harmony in your feet comes with realization. The more frequently this spiritual medicine is used, the sooner comes manifestation of perfect health." Surely a soothing, restful suggestion,—and please note the *repetition.*

The following "healing affirmation" was used by a certain cult at its regular meetings, the congregation repeating the words after the leader: "With reverent recognition of my birthright, I claim my sonship with the Almighty. I am free from disease and disorder. I am in harmony with my Source. The Infinite Health is made manifest in me. The Infinite

Substance is my constant supply. The Infinite Life fills and strengthens me. The Infinite Intelligence illumines and directs me. The Infinite Love surrounds and protects me. The Infinite Power upholds and supports me. I am out of bondage. I have the freedom of the Sons of God. With all that is in me, I rejoice and give thanks. God and men are the all in all, now and evermore." It may be seen that the above "affirmation," made slowly and solemnly, accompanied by the religious environment, is calculated to bring relief mental and physical. But still it is Suggestion.

The following "treatment" has been used for Constipation, and Delayed Menstruation, by one of the cults: "All the natural channels of my body are open and free. The substance of my body is good." The following "treatment" for General Health is used by one of the cults: "What is true of God is true of man. God is the One All, and is always in a state of wholeness. I, the man of God, am always whole, like unto the One-All. No false belief environs or limits me. No shadow darkens my mental vision. My body is a heavenly body, and my eyes do behold the glory of God in all visible things. I am well, and provided for, thank God, and nothing can make me think otherwise.'' The student of Suggestion recognizes and acknowledges the effect of similar suggestions upon those whose temperament inclines them toward this form of treatment. The fact of the cure is understood and admitted, while the theory is also understood.

The Emmanuel Movement uses similar ''treatments,'' but unlike the cults and metaphysical schools, or many of them, it freely admits the nature of the force used. It acknowledges Suggestion, instead of denying it. It says, practically, ''The healing power is inherent in the patient; Suggestion is the method of employing that power; and our treatments are among the better ways of arousing that power.''

Other cults and schools pursue the radical method of instructing the patient to *deny absolutely* the existence of the disease, pain or disorder. The theory is that as God is Good, and as all things come from God—therefore anything that is *not* Good cannot come from God, and therefore must be a false belief or illusion. The ''treatment'' consists in denying away or repudiating the "false belief," "error" or "claim" of the mortal mind. Without entering into a discussion of the metaphysical, or theological points mentioned, the student of Suggestion sees that these "denials" of the trouble, and the "affirmations" of health and wholeness, must exert a mighty suggestive effect upon the patient who believes. Fear is removed, and Hope takes its place. These treatments have a well recognized value in the catagory of Suggestion, in spite of the theories and dogmatic conceptions of the cults and schools employing them.

The student of Suggestion perceives, very soon, that anything that tends to produce a hopeful, optimistic mental attitude, in place of the mental state of fear, pessimism and despair, has a decided therapeutic value along the lines of Suggestion. Fear is a negative mental state and is recognized as a powerful depressant of the physical activities. Hope is most positive, and is a mighty invigorant of the physical activities. Confident Expectation is a mental state móst conducive to a manifestation of the desired and hoped-for physical condition. Any system of *materia*

medica, metaphysics, or religion, which is able
to let in the sunshine of Hope, Optimism and
Confident Expectation of Good, and which
thus drives out the darkness of Fear, Pessi-
misim and Confident Expectation of Evil—
has an important place in the category of Suggestive Therapeutics, no matter under what
name it may masquerade, or upon what theories, beliefs, dogmas, or ideas it may rest.
Its pragmatic value is determined by "What
does it do—how does it work—how does it
'make good' in action?"

CHAPTER XIV.

In contrast with the practitioners of Suggestive Therapeutics who give their suggestions under the forms and by the methods of the various metaphysical cults on the one hand, and those who give "masked suggestions" in the shape of *placebos,* harmless drugs, etc., on the other hand, there is to be found a large and constantly increasing number of practitioners who confine themselves to the practice of Suggestive Therapeutics, pure and simple. While the various methods of applying Suggestion varies according to the respective views of the practitioner, still there is to be found a general underlying basis of application in all of such cases. We shall now ask you to consider the general method of suggestive treatment followed by this school of healing.

In the first place the practitioner of Suggestive Therapeutics, pure and simple, does not attempt to "deny" the existence of the disease or disorder. Nor does he claim that the cure is due to any occult power or metaphysical belief. On the contrary, he bases his treatment upon the recognized laws of psychology, and physiology. He first endeavors to diagnose the cause of the trouble—not the symptoms, but the *cause.* This step being accomplished, he then endeavors to gain the confidence of the patient by a careful talk, and then directs his suggestions in such a way as to bring about a return of normal functioning of the cells, organs and parts of the patient. In order to do this he forms the mental image of *the healthy individual*, and endeavor to bring up the patient to that ideal. Instead of studying diseased conditions, he studies the conditions of normal health and then tries to bring up the patient to that standard by an appropriate line of Suggestion.

This process is not so intricate as it might appear at first thought, for, as a rule, the abnormal condition has been caused by a neglect of some of the rules and laws of normal living and thinking. A correction of these bad habits of living and thinking may be brought about by firm and repeated suggestions that the patient will act and think otherwise. In the majority of cases seeking suggestive treatment, there will be found a chronic condition of imperfect nutrition, digestion, assimilation, and elimination. This condition manifests itself in a poor circulation, weak digestion, nervousness, constipation, and general run down state of health. These cases are called "typical cases" requiring this form of treatment. The patient as a rule has a "weak stomach," cold hands and feet, poor circulation, nervousness, and is more or less constipated. If the patient is a woman, she is also apt to have menstrual troubles. In order to relieve this condition, the practitioner aims his suggestion directly toward starting correct habits of living, and in this way strikes right at the heart of the original cause of the trouble. Perhaps the best way to explain this to you, would be to give you a general outline of the treatment of a "typical case" of this kind, by a practitioner of Suggestive Therapeutics.

The treatment commences with a careful examination of the patient's condition; the securing of the history of the case; general symptoms, etc. This done, the practitioner tells the patient that he must not dwell upon the past history, nor upon the symptoms—he has come to a parting of the ways, and must "forget" the old troubles and leave them behind him. He then informs the patient that he must allow the suggestions to sink into his subconscious mind, there to take root and then manifest in physical conditions. Bidding the patient to assume a position of restful calm, he begins to give him suggestions, in a firm, quiet, but positive tone, with frequent repetitions of the vital points. The following will give a general idea of such a treatment:

"You are now resting, quietly and calmly, with a mind open to the inflow of strong, helpful suggestions, which will build you up gradually and surely into a condition of health. These suggestions will bring to your bodily cells and organs a normal healthy condition, in which they will be able to do the work that Nature intended them to do—and they *will* do it—they *will* do it. In the first place, we shall cause your stomach to act properly and digest the food that you place in it to nourish the body, and which shall be assimilated and distributed in the shape of rich good blood to

every part of your body—every part of your
body—there to do its work of building you up
—building you up to strong vigorous health.
You have cast aside all fear, and from now on
will look forward confidently and expectantly
toward the return of health. You will find
that your appetite for nourishing food is re-
turning—you will find that a normal healthy
hunger will return to you, beginning from this
minute. You will begin to crave nourishing
food, and such food will be well taken care of
by your digestive organs. You will masticate
your food thoroughly and slowly, thus gaining every particle of nourishment from it, and
rendering it easily digested—you will masticate your food thoroughly from now on. Your
saliva will prepare your food for your stomach, therefore you will masticate thoroughly
each mouthful of food that you eat hereafter
—each mouthful will be well masticated hereafter. Thus will you prepare it for the action
of the gastric juices which will flow freely in
your stomach, from now on, and which will
thoroughly digest every particle of the good
nourishing food for which you are beginning
to hunger already. Your stomach is strong,

strong, strong—strong and able to take care of the good nourishing food that you shall give it hereafter, because you will be hungry for it. The stomach will digest this food thoroughly, and the nourishment therefrom will be thoroughly assimilated and converted into rich red good blood, which will be carried to all parts of your body—to all parts of your body, there to build you up—to build you up, to health and strength.

"The body is built up from the nourishment obtained from good healthy food, for which you now feel hungry, and which you will digest easily. From to-day you will find yourself eating and digesting like the normal healthy person—for you *are* that normal healthy person, from now on. You will increase in health and strength every day, from now on. You will drink a sufficient quantity of fluids each day, for Nature requires these fluids in order to provide the various liquids of the system—the blood, the gastric juices, and the bile—all these things mean that you must increase your fluids. You will increase your fluids until you will drink nearly two quarts of water during each twenty-four hours

—this is the normal amount for the healthy man or woman, and you will soon learn to *want* this quantity. You will also begin to breathe fully, drawing in a few deep breaths every few hours. The air provides oxygen which invigorates and purifies your blood as it passes through your lungs. You will find that this deep breathing will make you feel strong and vigorous. You will find that you will begin to take a new interest in life, and will want to walk in the fresh air as Nature intended you to do. You will find that the increased fluids will tend to restore a normal movement of the bowels, and from now on you will be regular and natural in this respect. Your nerves will grow strong, and you will feel young and vigorous, and full of life. In short, from now on, you will begin to grow steadily and surely to be *a healthy human being,* such as Nature intended you to be. This is your birthright, and you are now going to claim your own. Health is the natural state, and you are going to be natural from now on. You will throw aside all worry and fear, and from now on will become a healthy, cheerful, bright and happy person.''

In the case of a woman patient, the suggestions also include normal functioning of the organs peculiar to the sex. In case of any special troubles, appropriate suggestions are also given, but in all cases the fundamental suggestions are included, for upon the restoration of natural normal functioning of the entire body depends perfect health, no matter what may be the special complaint.

In reading the above "typical treatment" the reader will be struck with the fact that these suggestions are all directed toward the conditions *which are desired*, rather than toward the eradication of the undesirable ones. This is in acordance with the fundamental principles of The New Psychology, which hold that negative conditions are best eradicated by the cultivation of the positive ones. Health is positive, disease negative—in building up the positive the negative disappears. Disease *is not a thing*—it is merely the negation of Health. Disease is like darkness, while Health is like light—turn on the light and the darkness has disappeared. This is the one great distinguishing feature of Suggestive Therapeutics—it looks toward the healthy condition, rather than upon the diseased ones. By keeping its eyes and thought fixed on the positive conditions, it tends to dissipate the negatives. The practitioner of Suggestive Therapeutics studies *the healthy man*, rather than the diseased one. His mind is ever filled with the thoughts of Health, and he endeavors to set up a corresponding mental image in the minds of his patients. He steadily refuses to even *talk* disease,—his talk is ever along the lines of health. The normal attracts him, not the abnormal. This in itself is a great step in advance in practice of any and all healing methods, and will undoubtedly be the "mental attitude" of practitioners of every school in the future.

It is impossible, of course, to give detailed instructions for treatment in a book of this kind, for such would be foreign to its general purpose. But, nevertheless, we have given you here the fundamentals of the best general treatment along the lines of Suggestive Therapeutics—you may alter, add, change, or modify them to meet the requirements of a variety of cases. The main point to be remembered is that confidence begets power, and that your suggestions should always be directed along the exact lines of physical change that you desire to produce. When you wish a boy to sit down, you bid him do so— follow the same plan in "talking to" the bodily organs, cells or parts. In this connection, read the next chapter.

CHAPTER XV.

"THE NEW METHOD."

In addition to the methods of applying Suggestive Therapeutics mentioned in the preceding chapters, in which the cells, organs and parts of the body are reached through the general subconscious mind of the patient, there is another form in which the suggestions are directed immediately to the cells themselves. This method while far from being favored by the majority of the authorities on the subject, and open to the objection of being but "masked suggestion" in which the apparent direct application is by a fanciful form of arousing the activities of the cells via the subconscious mind, nevertheless has attracted great attention from a number of earnest experimenters who have obtained very satisfactory results through it, and is therefore worthy of respectful consideration.

The theory underlying this direct method of applying Suggestion to the cells and organs, is based upon the general working hypothesis of the existence of mind in the cells and parts, which "mind" is capable of becoming aware of the desire, will or mental pictures (or whatever we choose to call it) in the mind of the person giving the suggestions. In other words the cells or parts may be made "conscious of" or "aware of" the state of mind of the suggester. It is not necessary to indulge in any special metaphysical theory or belief regarding the nature of these "cellminds," in order to practice this form of healing. It is sufficient for the purpose to rest content with the pragmatic idea that "it works"—that is, that the application of the method in question tends to arouse the cells, organs or parts in renewed activity and normal functioning. While the effect of this method of Suggestion is heightened by the employment of words, it is not necessary to assume that the cells or organs "understand" the words—the probability is that the words serve merely to intensify the mental state of the suggester, and to enable him to concentrate his mind upon his work.

But whatever may be the explanation of the method or means whereby the cells, organs or parts become "aware" of the intentions and desires of the suggester, experiments seem to show that they *do become aware* of the same, and respond thereto in varying degrees. Moreover, the cells, organs and parts seem capable of being trained to become sensible of the suggestions, and to respond thereto in a greater measure. Waiving all theories or "explanations," it may be said that the cells, organs and parts of the body *act as if they were aware* of the treatment being given them, and the suggestions being directed to them. Whether we assume that there is a direct channel of communication between the mind of the suggester and the cells, organs or parts; or whether we fall back upon the idea that the channel is really through the general subconsciousness and that the direct suggestions operate merely as a striking method of applying Suggestion through the ordinary channels, the fact remains that in giving and taking these treatments excellent results may be obtained by assuming, even conditionally, that the cells, organs or parts are "entities" capable of understanding the suggestions and responding thereto. And, whatever may be the details of the real reason of the process, the general fact remains that there *is* mind in the cells, organs and parts, that is somehow, someway, aroused and which responds to the suggestive influence.

The method of application of this form of Suggestion is simplicity itself. All that is necessary is that the suggester arouse the attention of the cells, and then address them as if they were entities. These cells or organ entities vary in degree of "intelligence," not only so far as is concerned the differences between the personality of their owners, but also in the matter of differences in themselves. The cells in the liver differ from the cells in the heart or stomach for instance. These cell-minds resemble the minds of children—very young children, in fact. There must be something done to arouse their attention, and then to hold their interest. This being done, they must be "spoken to" authoritatively, and firmly, with constant repetition and insistence. They must be told what to do, and they must be held up to their work by insistent command and demand. The successful practitioner of this form of Suggestion must needs possess

and display many of the characteristics of the
successful school-teacher of the lower grades.
In an earlier work on this subject, we said:
"The way to reach the mind in the cells, cell-
groups, ganglia, organs, nerves, parts, etc.,
of the body, is to *address yourself directly to
it, just as you would to a person.* You must
think of the mind in the affected part, as a
'person' who is misbehaving. You must re-
monstrate with, argue with, coax, order, or
'drive' the 'person' residing in the organ, just
as you would different individuals. Sometimes coaxing is much better than driving, and
sometimes the forceful method is necessary,
as we shall see. You may either talk aloud to
the mind in the organ, or else (and this is the
better way in treating others) you may do
your talking mentally. Tell the cell-mind just
what you expect of it—just what you intend it
shall do—just what is right for it to do, etc.
And it will obey." In this statement is contained the essence of this method of applying
Suggestion. The rest is merely a matter of
detail.

In this form of treatment, many practitioners begin by using the hands to tap lightly

or sharply over the affected organ or part,
which seems to arouse something akin to attention. This seems to be needed particularly
at first until the cells "get used to you." The
idea seems to be akin to that put into effect
when we tap a man on the arm or shoulder, to
attract his attention from the many sights and
sounds around him. It is as if we tapped over
the organ, saying "Here you! Wake up!
Listen to me!" in a firm authoritative manner.
It is like the tap of the gavel on the speaker's
desk in Congress—or the tapping of the teacher's gong in school—or the military command of "Attention!" It operates precisely
in the same way, and in the same way there is
noticed an acquiring of the habit of coming
to attention on the part of the organ or cells,
after a few treatments. Personally, we are of
the opinion that the use of the hands in certain forms of treatment has a similar effect,
and that much of the after details of these
various manual treatments act along the lines
of Suggestion.

After having aroused the attention of the
cell, organ or part, the suggester proceeds to
"talk to" it, using forcible suggestions. Quot-

ing from our former work referred to: "A plain, simple way of giving this treatment is to awaken the attention of the mind in the cell, organ or part, as above stated, and then proceeding to mentally lecture it, calling it by name, as for instance: 'Here, Stomach!' or 'Now, you Liver!' etc. Don't smile at this advice—just try it on yourself, and you will stop smiling. *Then go on and tell the Organ-Mind just what you would tell it if it were an actual personality—a childish mind for instance.* You will soon find how quick the organ-mind is to awaken to your words, and to act upon your suggestions or orders. Follow the law of Suggestion in giving these treatments to the organ-minds—that is, remember the suggestive phases of Repetition, Authoritative Demand or Command, etc. Don't be afraid, but start in to give the Organ-Mind a 'piece of your mind,' and it will obey you. . . . There are no fixed forms of treatment along these lines. You must acquire the 'knack' by practice. The proper words will suggest themselves to you. The thing to do is to know what you want done, and then to command the organ-mind to do that thing; using the same words that you would use in talking to a real person in the place of the organ. You will soon acquire the art, by a little practice. Those who have treated a large number of persons in this way have told me that the mind in the organs and parts seem to instinctively recognize the healer's power over them. Just as a horse or dog will recognize men who are accustomed to managing animals of their kind, so will these organ-minds recognize their master in one who has practiced the art of healing along these lines.''

All who have practiced this form of Suggestive Healing, bear testimony to the fact that there are great differences in the degrees of ''intelligence'' in the various organs, and also great differences in the ''nature or disposition'' of the various organs. For instance, the heart is found to be quite ''intelligent'' and amenable to reasonable suggestion, encouragement and control. The liver, on the contrary, is always found to be a heavy, sluggish, stubborn, mulish, obstinate entity, which yields only to sharp and vigorous commands and driving. 'As one person once said to us: ''The liver is a mule, and must be treated as such"—and we agree perfectly with this statement. There is just as much difference between a spirited horse, and a mulish mule, as between the heart and the liver. Accordingly there must be a difference in the treatment applied to these parts. The one needs but a little gentle patting and urging, while the other needs "the big stick." The stomach occupies a position between the two—possibly the position of a draught-horse. When not brutalized with stuffing and over-work, the stomach is a very faithful, hard working organ. It has a tendency to become frightened at adverse suggestions, and is rendered weak by fear. But it may be encouraged and restored to normal functioning by this method of treatment. It responds to trust, encouragement and reassurance, and has a desire to perform tasks expected of it, if fear is taken away from it. A peculiar thing about the stomach is that it seems to like "jollying" or "flattery"—tell it how good a stomach it is, and how well it can do its work; and how much you trust it to run things right for you; and lo! it proceeds to make good, and to justify your praise and commendations.

The nerves respond readily to this form of treatment, along gentle coaxing lines. The circulation of the blood may be increased in certain parts, or restrained, in this way. In this way the blood may be swept all over the body, creating a pleasant glow; or it may be drawn away from an aching head, or a feverish brow. The bowels respond readily to a firm, kind treatment, in which they are told to move regularly—it being well to name a certain time at which you expect them to establish a regular habit, *in which case be sure to keep your appointment with them, and give them a chance.* The organs peculiar to women will respond readily to this form of treatment. Regular menstruation has often been established by treatments of this kind, given a month ahead, and keeping it up every day until the regular period—in this case the fixing of a date being an important detail. Suggestions of "Firm, now, firm and strong" have relieved many cases of weakness of the uterus. Profuse menstruation has yielded to the commands of 'Slow, now; easy; easy; not to free a flow' etc."

The method considered in this chapter may

be applied either along the lines of ordinary
Suggestion given by one person to another;
or along the lines of Auto-Suggestion or self-
treatment, in which the suggestions are given
by the person himself direct to the minds in
the cells, organs or parts—just as if one were
treating another person.

PART III

AUTO-SUGGESTION

CHAPTER XVI.

By "Auto-Suggestion" is meant the application of the principles of Suggestion *by oneself upon oneself.* In Auto Suggestion the individual plays the dual role of suggester and suggestee, respectively. In all other respects it is precisely the same thing as Suggestion in its general phases. In Auto-Suggestion may be found the Suggestion of Impression, the Suggestion of Induction, the Suggestion of Association, which are found in the ordinary phases of Suggestion. In Auto-Suggestion may be noticed the five phases of Suggestion, viz: Suggestion of Authority, Suggestion of Association, Suggestion of Habit, Suggestion of Repetition and Suggestion of Imitation, respectively.

It may seem strange to think of one's suggesting to oneself "with authority," but it is true that if one will use the authority of his will he may impress upon his subconsciousness such suggestions as he may wish to place there, and may thus *make over his entire character,* or develop within himself the qualities which he may desire. In the same way he may force associations upon his mind by Suggestion, and thus produce the same effect upon himself as those produced by associative suggestions from without. One may suggest habits of thought, action and feeling upon himself, just as truly as habits may be induced by suggestions from without. As for the Suggestion of Repetition, it will be found that this phase of Suggestion plays a most important part in Auto-Suggestion. Even Suggestion of Imitation plays its part in Auto-Suggestion, for one may suggest to himself that he will imitate others; emulate them; pattern after them; model upon them; if he so desires. In short, in Auto-Suggestion we find that we have Suggestion in all of its many phases and forms, the only difference being that the individual gives the suggestions to himself, instead of receiving them from outside sources. The study of Auto-Suggestion is really the study of Suggestion.

Those authorities in The New Psychology who analyze things to their ultimate elements, rightly hold that the active principle of all Suggestion is really Auto-Suggestion. That is to say, that the active force manifested in Suggestion, is really called into play by the individual himself, usually involuntarily. When we accept a suggestion from outside, we allow it to pass the portals of our reason and judgment into the workshop of our will, there to set into motion the machinery of our mind. We allow our reason and judgment to neglect their duty, and to thereby admit undesirable strangers to our mental workshop. In Auto-Suggestion, as the term is generally applied, we voluntarily select and choose the suggestions which we wish to impress us, and we add to their effect by repetition and attention. But in both Suggestion and Auto-Suggestion the principle employed is precisely the same. The power is entirely within the mind of the person himself, although it may require the assistance of some outside person to call it into effect. The Suggestionist drives away fear and inspires confidence and expectant attention, and then leads and directs the will of the patient in the direction of performing the physical cure. Or he uses Suggestion in one or more of its phases, in order to induce the person to accept and believe what he says or does, and thereby gains the same effect as if the person had reasoned out the matter and impressed it upon his own mind. Suggestion from outside is the use by another of one's mental tools and machinery; while Auto-Suggestion is the use of the same tools and machinery by oneself.

It is difficult to draw a dividing-line between the phenomena of Suggestion and that of Auto-Suggestion—they blend into each other in many subtle degrees. For instance, one may receive an impression from outside —an impression which is the effect of a suggestion from outside—and being impressed by it, he may think it over and think and feel about it, so that the idea takes a firm hold upon him. Up to this point it is Suggestion in its general phase. But, then he repeats the suggestion to himself, both in self-communion and in conversation with others, until he has made an impression much deeper than that caused by the original impression. This secondary effect is Auto-Suggestion, of course.

There is another form of Auto-Suggestion

which is overlooked by many of the authorities. We refer to cases of involuntary Auto-Suggestion—cases in which the person impresses suggestions upon himself without intending to do so. We may illustrate this last mentioned phase by the tale of the man who tells a "fish-story" so often that he gets to believe it himself. Although the story may have had but little basis in fact, the constant, earnest repetition of it with the intention of impressing it upon others, acts as a repeated Auto-Suggestion which impresses itself upon the subconscious mind until it becomes a fixture there. Everyone who reads these words will be able to recall cases of this kind in his own experience.

The above mentioned form of Auto-Suggestion finds an illustration in the cases of many men whose business or profession finds them engaged in exploiting certain sophistries or half-truths, which are so known to them in the beginning—these tales told repeatedly for a period of time become actual truths to these persons by reason of Auto-Suggestion, and they fall victims to their own suggestive power. There are many instances of charlatans and religious imposters who finally fell victims to their own repeated suggestions, coming to actually believe the tales which they invented to impress others. We have a personal knowledge of a case in which an owner of a celebrated patent medicine purporting to cure nervousness, and who wrote his own startling advertisements in which he claimed all symptoms as indicating "nervousness," finally falling a victim to his own suggestive imagination and becoming a hypochondriac filled with fears of "symptoms" and possessed with the idea that he was a nervous wreck.

We believe that a celebrated religious imposter, now dead, fell a victom to his own claims of divine inspiration and power, and became mentally unbalanced by reason thereof. In fact, it is a common and well-known fact in the history of "new religions" that many of the leaders of such movements become mentally unbalanced by the constant repetition of their tales of "inspiration," "special divine guidance" and the rest of it. Writers along special lines often have a hard fight to avoid being overcome with the Auto-

Suggestions made easy by reason of their constant statements of certain special things. Experts on insanity frequently become insane. Writers upon certain forms of disease are often affected by their own statements, constantly repeated. Salesmen become impressed with certain tales told about their particular goods, that if they happen to change employers the old Auto-Suggestions are very hard to overcome. Fanaticism and bigotry arise often from the constant statement of certain beliefs to others, acting as Auto-Suggestion. In short, that which we constantly repeat to ourselves, and others, tends to become a fixed impression in our minds, difficult to eradicate, and often influencing us to a great extent. This being the case, we should avoid influencing ourselves along these undesirable lines, and should always try to impress ourselves with desirable qualities and ideas. We have the power of intelligent choice in this matter—there is no excuse for not using it properly.

Many of the cures claimed by Suggestion in its many forms, are really due to the Auto-Suggestion of the patient, pure and simple. Of course *all* mental cures have the element of Auto-Suggestion largely in evidence, but in some cases we can say that Auto-Suggestion does *all* the work. For instance, we have frequently heard mental healers relate cases in which patients wrote to them for "absent treatment," and received results even before the healer received the letter requesting treatment. Leaving out of the question, entirely, all discussion of the virtues, merits and explanation of "absent treatments," it must be admitted that in the cases mentioned *there was no "absent treatment" whatsoever* at the time, and that the entire benefit arose from the Auto-Suggestion of the patient. In one case the healer tells that the patient's original letter was misdirected and went astray, and that the first that the healer knew of the matter was the receipt of a second letter, a month later, in which the patient testified to the wonderful effect of the "month's treatments" that she supposed she was receiving. The cure was not an imaginary one either, for investigation revealed a case in which the physicians held that there was a chronic condition beyond cure, and that the patient had been perfectly restored to health.

Of course, we have heard of "explanations" of these cures, to the effect that in some way the "subjective mind" of the patient seeks the "subjective mind" of the healer, in the ether, and there receives the "treatment." This may be all true—we cannot prove that it is not; but Auto-Suggestion affords a much simpler explanation. If the patient had pinned her faith on the bones of St. Anne, or some other object, to the same extent that she believed in the healer, she would have received the same result—all experience and investigation proves this. These cases bear all the evidences of cases of Auto-Suggestion.

In this connection, we may add that the recital of these cases, and the "subjective mind meeting" in the ether, has injured the business of certain absent healers, for their patients finding that they can receive this "subjective mind" treatment without paying for it in the regular way, now do not write to the healers at all, but simply make the "etheric" connection, and receive the treatment (?) free of charge and without the knowledge of the healers. Surely this is a case of psychic "wire-tapping" needing the attention of the authorities! To the student of Auto-Suggestion all of these wonderful things are found to be very simple at the last analysis, and to rest upon the firm foundation of pure psychology. And in the same category may be placed the strange cases which the scoffing public would dismiss as "only imagination." Auto-Suggestion is a potent force, which works great harm to persons who misuse it, or who use it ignorantly; but which is equally potent for good when rightly and intelligently employed. It is a most valuable mental instrument or tool, with which we may make of ourselves what we will. It lies very close to the heart of The New Psychology.

CHAPTER XVII.

SELF-IMPRESSION.

'As we have said in the preceding chapter, the person practicing Auto-Suggestion is both the suggester and suggestee. He plays a dual role, viz (1) the part of the teacher or master; and (2) the part of the pupil or scholar. Auto-Suggestion might well be called "Self Impression," for the latter term correctly describes the actual process. The objective "I" impresses the subjective "Me." The conscious region of the mind impresses the subconsciousness. This is the whole thing in a nutshell. The actual process is a case of "Sez I to meself, sez I."

It is astonishing how the subconscious mind may be trained to work for one by a scientific course of Auto-Suggestion or Self-Impression. 'As we have said in a previous work on the subject: "One may charge his subconscious mind with the task of waking him up at a certain time in the morning—and he wakes up. Or he may charge his mind to remember a certain thing—and he remembers it. This form of self-mastery may be carried to great lengths, and one may bid his subconscious mind collect data regarding certain subjects, from amidst its heterogeneous collection of mental odds and ends of knowledge; and then bid it combine the information into a systematic form—and the mind will so act, and the combined information will be at hand when needed. I find myself doing this, almost unconsciously, when I start to write a book—fact after fact, and illustration after illustration, appearing at their proper time and place. The field of Self-Impression or Auto-Suggestion, and the workings of the subconscious mind, have just had their outer edges explored—there is a great field of mentation here awaiting some of you."

Auto-Suggestion may be considered in several phases, although the underlying principle is the same. In the first place every person has filled his mind with a number of involuntary Auto-Suggestions arising from the repetition of suggestions and impressions originally received from outward sources. These Auto-Suggestions are harbored in the shape of prejudices for and against persons or things; certain fixed beliefs not based upon reason or actual judgment or experience; certain arbitrary associations; and other results of previous impressions which have become firmly fixed by repetition along the lines of Auto-Suggestion.

Another phase is that in which the Auto-Suggestion is given and accepted tacitly or by implication, as when one takes a certain medicine believing that it will produce a certain result, in which the suggestion is transformed into Auto-Suggestion by the belief of the person. For instance if your friend gives you a powder saying that it will tend toward improved digestion, and you believe him—then when you take the powder you will have the following idea: "This powder will settle my stomach and cause me to digest my dinner perfectly." Although the idea may not be uttered in spoken words, nevertheless there will be the verbal Auto-Suggestion. In the same way you may give yourself an implied adverse Auto-Suggestion regarding fresh air, or certain foods, and the result is that you experience a bad effect. This form of Auto-Suggestion consists in a *firm belief* on your part that certain things will produce certain results, or that certain things possess certain qualities, etc. Every one has a goodly stock of Auto-Suggestions of this type, which exert a greater or less effect upon his character and actions. Carried to extreme, they produce fanaticism, bigotry, fixed-ideas or even monomania. Lacking them, the person is apt to be more or less fickle, unsettled, changeable and uncertain. Much that we have called "principles" of conduct is based upon this type of Auto-Suggestion heightened by habit. The moral is obvious.

The third type or class of Auto-Suggestion is that form of impression which is deliberately and voluntarily impressed upon the subconscious mind by the conscious mind, with and for a particular definite purpose. For instance, you wish to catch a train tomorrow morning shortly after four o'clock; you deliberately charge your subconscious mind with the idea "awake at four o'clock to catch that train," and you find that you will awake from your sleep about that time. You "have it on your mind," and you awake. The subconscious mind may be set like an alarm clock. In the same way a mother's subconscious mind will cause her to awaken at the slightest noise of the babe, while much louder noises will fail to arouse her. You have an engagement at three o'clock, and charge your mind with it, and a little before the hour you will find a certain mental uneasiness manifesting itself, and just before the hour the thought will flash into your conscious field of mind: "That engagement with Smith at three o'clock." It is this phase of Suggestion that is actively employed in the Character Building processes which form so important a part in the practical work of The New Psychology. The New Psychology teaches that one may build up any set of brain-cells by appropriate lines of Auto-Suggestion and resulting action, which will develop certain desired tendencies and characteristics. Also one may inhibit or neutralize certain objectionable traits or characteristics by deliberately building up the qualities directly opposed to those of which he desires to be rid. There is nothing occult or mystical about this process—it is based upon the scientific knowledge of the mind and brain.

This last mentioned phase of Auto-Suggestion plays an important part in the methods and practices of the many metaphysical cults and schools, including those of religious cults which use similar methods. The various "affirmations," "denials," "statements," etc., used by these cults and schools are but forms of Auto-Suggestion, and their results are obtained along its lines. Much good work has been accomplished by these organizations and schools in the direction of producing improved mental, physical and moral conditions. Many a person has been brought out of enfeebled and abnormal physical conditions; many a one has changed his mental states and character of thought; many a person's moral character has been improved by these methods. In spite of the extravagant statements and claims of some of the cults, there has been a great deal of good accomplished by them. They have replaced Pessimism with Optimism; Fear with Hope; Despair with Courage. But it is not necessary to accept any of their theories, dogmas, or creeds, in order to partake of the benefits of the "treatments," for an understanding of

Auto-Suggestion, and an intelligent practicing of its methods will enable any one to secure these beneficial results along purely scientific lines.

The one possible weak point of the various methods of applying Auto-Suggestion, and one which has not escaped the attention of the critics, is that unless the person understands the underlying principles, there is a tendency toward resting content with the mere "lip statement" of the Auto-Suggestion, and a neglect to manifest into activity and actual "doing" the desired quality or power. In the following chapters we shall endeavor to point out an improved plan of applying Auto-Suggestion, in which there is employed a correlated physical activity in connection with the use of the proper Auto-Suggestion.

To those who are repelled by the vague metaphysical conception of the cults, and who, while desirous of obtaining the benefits of the methods of Auto-Suggestion, demand some explanation along purely material lines, we would say that a little examination into the teachings of science regarding the nature and function of the brain will explain the work-

ing principle of Auto-Suggestion, along purely physical lines and without recourse to metaphysical theory. Science informs us that the
brain is composed of a substance called
"plasm," which consists of an enormous
number of tiny cells which are used in the
manifestation of thought. These brain-
cells are estimated to number from 500,000,-
000 to 2,000,000,000, according to the mental
activity of the individual. There is always
a great number of reserve brain-cells remaining unused in every brain, the estimate being
that even in the case of the most active brain
there are always several millions of reserve
brain-cells at any time. Science also informs
us that the brain grows additional brain-cells
to meet an increased demand. Brain-building
consists of the development and growth of
brain-cells in any special region of the brain,
for the brain consists of various centres and
localities, in which are manifested the various
mental faculties, qualities or functions. By
developing the brain-cells in any particular
region, the quality, activity, or faculty which
has that region for its seat is necessarily
greatly increased and rendered more effective

and powerful. It is a fully demonstrated scientific fact that man may "make himself over" mentally, if he will but devote the same degree of attention, patience and work to the subject that he would in case of desired development of some part of the physical body— some muscle or limb, for instance. And the processes are almost identical in the case of muscle and brain-cells—use, exercise, and practice along the lines of Auto-Suggestion and its correlated activities.

CHAPTER XVIII.

The majority of writers and teachers of Auto-Suggestion confine themselves to methods similar to those of the cults and metaphysical schools, inasmuch as their methods consist almost entirely of certain more or less well-selected "affirmations," "statements," or auto-suggestions, which the person is expected to repeat to himself, with the idea of thereby impressing upon his subconscious mentality the idea back of the words. This, of course, is an important part of the true method of Auto-Suggestion, but there are other features to be included in order to obtain the best results. There is the danger of one becoming mechanical in the automatic statements of "I am *this*" or "I am *that*" of the affirmative methods. There is the tendency of the habit-mind to take up the affirmations or statements and to continue the repetition along automatic lines, similar to the meaningless repetitions of the parrot, or the mechanical repetitions of the phonograph. In this way the affirmations fail to carry their dynamic force to the subconscious mind, and consequently the impressions cease to be clearly and distinctly made. The process becoming mere habit, is like the phenomenon of the mind refusing to be impressed by a continuous accustomed noise or sound, while alive to any variation therefrom. The affirmations must be made in a manner which will hold the attention and interest, and must also be accompanied by correlated actions, in order to become fully effective in the work of character building. There must be a seeing and doing, as well as a *saying*. The best impressions are made by (1) Saying; (2) Seeing; and (3) Acting and Doing. Let us consider this threefold method.

In the first place, we have always contended that there is a much better way of *saying*, or speaking the affirmation or auto-suggestion, than the familiar "I am *this*, or *that*." We have found that the nearer one comes to the perfect playing out of the dual role of suggester and suggestee, the better will be the result—the clearer will be the impression upon the subconscious mind. Accordingly one should endeavor to "talk to himself" as if he were speaking to another person. He should endeavor to give his suggestions to himself, precisely as if he were suggesting to another person. Whatever may be the detail of the psychic operation, the fact remains that by so doing he will be able to obtain and register a much clearer, deeper and more lasting impression than by the "I am this, or that" form of affirmation. In fact, we think that the idea of "affirmation" may as well be discarded, first and last, in the practical work of Auto-Suggestion, and that the "I" of the person should actually *suggest* to the "Me" of himself. Let it be Suggestion, instead of *affirmation.*

In making these suggestions to yourself, you should always address yourself (when giving the suggestions) *as if you were speaking to a third person.* Instead of saying "I am courageous and fearless," you should suggest to yourself as follows: "John Smith, (here use your own name, of course), John Smith you are courageous and fearless; you fear nothing; every day you are gaining in courage and fearlessness, and are getting stronger, stronger, stronger, etc." Do you get the idea? Try both methods now—stopping your reading for the purpose. Say as strong an "I am" as you can, and then try the effect of the strongest suggestion of "You are" addressed to your subconsciousness. Imagine that you are suggesting to another person whom you are very desirous of building up and strengthening. You will find a new field of Auto-Suggestion opening up before you. A little knack is required, but a few trials will show you the value of this improved method. Talk to "John Smith" as if he were an entirely different individual. Tell him what you wish him to do and become, and how you expect him to act. You will be surprised to see how obedient this subconscious mentality will become.

The following illustration, taken from one of our earlier works, will give you the idea of a "sample" treatment by Auto-Suggestion: "Suppose you wish to cultivate Fearlessness in place of the Fearthought that has bothered you so much, . . . you wish to use Auto-Suggestion. The old way, you remember,

was to claim to yourself 'I am Fearless, etc.'
The new way of treating yourself is to imagine that you are giving a suggestive treatment to some other person, for precisely the
same trouble. Sit down and give a regular
treatment *to yourself,* imagining that you, the
individual, are giving a treatment to the
"Me" or personality—the Central Mind giving a treatment to the John Smith part of you,
the personality. Do you see? The Individual (that's *You*) says to the personality of
'John Smith' (your subconscious self) : 'Here,
John Smith, you must brace up and do better.
You are fearless, fearless, fearless! I tell you,
you are fearless! You are courageous, brave
and bold! You fear nothing! You are confident and self-reliant! You are filled with
strong, positive mind-power, and you are going to manifest it—you are going to grow
more and more positive every day! You are
positive this minute—do you hear me?
POSITIVE this very minute, I say; positive
this very minute! You are positive, fearless,
confident, and self-reliant, right now, and you
will grow more and more so every day. Remember now, you are positive, positive, posi-

tive—fearless, fearless, fearless' etc., etc., etc. You will find that by this plan you will be able fairly to pour the positive suggestions into the receptive subconscious mind—and that the 'John Smith' part of you will accept the impressions just as if there were two persons instead of one." This is not childish nor mere play—it is a process based upon the soundest psychological principles. You will be surprised to find how readily you may "order yourself around" by following this plan for a while.

In the succeeding chapter, we will give you some Auto-Suggestions for specific cases, to be used along the above lines. Acquire the knack of suggesting to yourself, and you will have a great work of self-improvement opened out for you.

The second step in the improved method of Auto-Suggestion, consists of what has been called "Visualization," which consists of forming the mental image of yourself as possessed of the qualities which you wish to develop in yourself. The clearer mental picture that you can make of yourself, *as you wish to be,* the deeper and clearer impression will be made by the accompanying Auto-Suggestion. The explanation of this lies in the fact that *ideals tend to materialize objectively.* It is a psychological fact that we tend to grow toward our ideals. An ideal is a mental pattern upon which is modeled our character, actions, and general life. Many a man has attained success in life by his faithful adherance to some great ideal held firmly in his mind. The thing that fills our mental eye is the thing towards which we move. This is recognized in all moral teaching and religion, although the psychological principle is not understood. The young are taught to take some great example as an ideal—some great figure in religious or secular history. The Christian is taught to model his life upon that great ideal of the character of the founder of his faith. The Catholic child is also taught to consider the lives of the saints, and the devout fathers of the church. It is so in all religions, and forms one of the great incentives of religious life. Our school children are directed to the lives of Washington, Lincoln, and other patriots. The model of the private life of Queen Victoria inspired English social

life for over half-a-century, and its effect
still persists. The Swiss have been inspired by
the ideal of William Tell. The Japanese national ideal acts in the direction of a positive
inspiraton to the young men of that land.
Nations like individuals, incline toward their
ideals. And this is the "reason" of our advising you to idealize yourself, in a visualized
mental image of yourself *as you wish to be.*
Hold firmly to your ideal, and you will grow
like it—the material manifestation follows
upon the mental idealization.

The third phase of this method of Auto-
Suggestion consists in "acting out" the part
in which you wish to become perfect. Not
only do you thus gain the benefit of practice,
and repetitive suggestion, in the manner of a
rehearsal—but there is also a psychological
law involved in this phase. Just as thought
tends to take form in action, so does action
tend to react upon thought. Let us quote from
a few authorities on this subject. Prof. Halleck says: "By restraining the expression of
an emotion we can frequently throttle it; by
inducing the expression of an emotion we can
often cause its allied emotion." Prof. Wm.

James says: "Refuse to express a passion, and it dies. Count ten before venting your anger, and its occasion seems ridiculous. Whistling to keep up courage is no mere figure of speech. On the other hand, sit all day in a moping posture, sigh and reply to everything in a dismal voice, and your melancholy lingers. There is no more valuable precept in moral education than this, as all of us who have experienced know: If we wish to conquer undesirable emotional tendencies in ourselves we must assiduously, and in the first instance cold-bloodedly, *go through the outward movements* of those contrary dispositions which we wish to cultivate. Smooth the brow, brighten the eye, contract the dorsal rather than the ventral aspect of the frame, and speak in a major key, pass the genial compliment, and your heart must indeed be frigid if it does not gradually thaw."

The following quotation from a recent article of Dr. Woods Hutchinson throws light on this question of the reaction of physical states upon mental conditions, moods and character:

"To what extent muscular contractions condition emotions, as Prof. James has sug-

gested, may be easily tested by a quaint and
simple little experiment upon a group of the
smallest voluntary muscles in the body, those
that move the eyeball. Choose some time
when you are sitting quietly in your room,
free from all disturbing thoughts and influences. Then stand up, and assuming an easy
position, cast the eyes upward and hold them
in that position for thirty seconds. Instantly
and involuntarily you will be conscious of a
tendency toward reverential, devotional, con-
templative ideas and thoughts. Then turn
the eyes sideways, glancing directly to the
right or to the left, through half-closed lids.
Within thirty seconds images of suspicion, of
uneasiness, or of dislike will rise unbidden in
the mind. Turn the eyes on one side and
slightly downward, and suggestions of jealousy or coquetry will be apt to spring unbidden. Direct your gaze downward toward the
floor, and you are likely to go off into a fit of
reverie or of abstraction.'' Bain says: ''Most
of our emotions are so closely connected with
their expression that they hardly exist if the
body remains passive.'' Maudsley says:
''The specific muscular action is not merely

an exponent of passion, but truly an essential part of it. If we try while the features are fixed in the expression of one passion to call up in the mind a different one, we shall find it impossible to do so.''

In view of the above facts, do you not see why it is important that *action* should be added to saying and seeing, in Auto-Suggestion? Lose no opportunity to act out the part into which you wish to grow. Manifest into action, as frequently as possible, the qualities which you wish to make your own, and in which you wish to develop. Exercise, exercise, exercise; practice, practice, practice; rehearse, rehearse, rehearse! Let your thought manifest and take form in action, for not only do you develop the thought and idea by so doing, but you will also gain the advantage of the reaction of the physical state upon the mental. If you walk down the street with clenched fists, you will soon begin to feel cross and combatitive. If you go about wearing a frown, you will soon experience a feeling of peevishness and irritability, and will manifest it toward those around. Wearing a smile causes the ''smile-feeling'' to come. It is action and reaction, always, between the physical and the mental. Take advantage of this law of life, and turn it to good account in your work of Auto-Suggestion.

In the advice given in the two succeeding chapters, be sure to remember that the *action* and the visualization must always accompany the verbal suggestions recommended to you. Do not be content with suggesting to yourself the qualities you wish to develop, but also visualize them as an ideal, and finally *act them out* in actual life as often as possible. Cultivate the physical characteristics accompanying the mental qualities you wish to develop or acquire. By acting out the qualities n private, you will ascertain just what these physical characteristics are—then practice hem until you make them your own, and then cquire the habit of manifesting them permanently. You will be surprised at the benfit of this reflex action, or reaction of the hysical upon the mental. This point is often verlooked by the teachers of Auto-Suggeson, but it is most important. We trust that ou will give to it the consideration that it erits.

CHAPTER XIX.

By "Character" we mean the personal qualities and attributes of a man or woman. It is significant that the Greek word from which the word arose signifies an impression as that of a seal or die. Character is really the result of impressions of some kind received by the mind or brain of the person. A person's character is the result of the various impressions that have been made upon it. Character may be moulded, shaped and changed by Auto-Suggestions along the lines mentioned in the preceding chapter—suggestion to oneself; mental imaging; and acting out the part.

In character-building the first thing is to take mental stock of oneself, so as to determine which traits should be inhibited, repressed or restrained and which should be developed. Every one knows his strong and weak points, but few lack the honesty to confess them to themselves. Enter into confession with yourself, and make a list of the traits which should be restrained, and those which should be developed. Then proceed to develop the desirable ones by the three-fold method; and restrain the undesirable ones by developing their opposites. Let us consider a few of these mental qualities, or characteristics, in order to get some light on the practical working of the method.

1. *Continuity.* This faculty or quality is that which regulates the degree of patient and persistent application to the thing before one. It is the "Stick-to-itive" faculty, which is so deficient in many people. Its cultivation is possible by the following Auto-Suggestion, accompanied by the appropriate mental pictures, and the appropriate action. Auto-Suggestion: "John Smith, you are developing Continuity; you are learning to apply yourself fixedly and firmly to the task before you; you are growing able to concentrate firmly upon one thing until you complete the task; you are growing to give your whole attention to the one thing before you, until it is finished; you are learning to keep up one train of thought until you have exhausted it; you are

finding it easier to do this, and easier to avoid scattering your mental energies—easier each day. You are acquiring a fixed purpose, and a strong concentration. You are growing strong in Continuity. You are developing the brain-centres which manifest Continuity," etc., etc. Accompany this with the mental picture of yourself practicing concentration and persistency, attention and application. Create the ideal of yourself as possessing and manifesting the quality in a high degree. Then endeavor to act out the part as much as possible. Practice with the things before you, and learn to manifest Continuity in your every-day life, allowing no opportunity to escape you. In case you wish to restrain the faculty, should you possess it in too strong a degree, reverse the process and model your method so as to develop the opposite quality—love of variety, diversity, etc.

2. *Combativeness.* This is the faculty of resistance, opposition, etc. Some have it in excess—some are deficient in it. To develop it, use the following Auto-Suggestion: "John Smith, you are learning to stand up for your rights; you are developing the power of right-

ful resistance; you are becoming more spirited and courageous every day; you are growing moral courage; you are sticking to what you believe are your rightful dues; you are standing up against oppression; you are developing the faculty of self-defense; you are learning to refuse to retreat; you are holding your own; you are developing the quality of 'let-me-alone;' you are cultivating the power to stand as firm as a rock against all opposition; you are learning to achieve, conquer, and win out,'' etc. Accompany this with the appropriate mental pictures, and the appropriate actions. Practice the desired qualities as often as possible. Develop your mental muscle. Stop being a worm of the dust, or human door-mat, and assert your individuality. If you possess this quality in too great a degree, restrain it by cultivating the opposite quality of live-and-let-live; forbearance; brotherly love; etc. The ideal condition is that which lies between the two extremes.

3. *Acquisitiveness.* This is the faculty which manifests in the securing and saving of money and things. Some possess it to an intolerable degree, while others are kept poor

all their lives from a lack of it. To develop this faculty, use the following Auto-Suggestion: "John Smith, you are getting over your foolishness; you are learning to desire money, and to want to save it; you are learning to *get* money and to *hold on* to it; you are developing the ability to get all that is coming to you, and to hold on to it after you get it; you are learning to be frugal and economical, and at the same time are developing the faculty of acquiring the good things of life. You need these things, and you are going to have them—you are beginning to set into operation the things which will bring you these things that you need and want, and you are learning how to hold on to them as they reach you," etc. Accompany this with the mental picture of yourself as "wanting what you want, and wanting it *now*;" of drawing to you from all sides the things you want; as having the things, and holding tight fast to them; see yourself as "having and holding," and as "letting nothing get away from you." Then manifest this thought in action; begin to reach out after the good things of life, *and hold fast to what you get*. Remember the

words of the song: "Every little bit, added to
what you've got, makes just a little bit more."
Demand your share of the opulence of the
world, and get it—then hold on to it. To
restrain this quality, develop its opposite—
begin to "loosen up," in thought, suggestion
and action.

4. *Secretiveness*. This is the faculty of
the closed-lips, and silent tongue, and the
avoidance of telling one's affairs to the world.
A certain amount of it is very desirable, for
many reasons; an excess of it tends toward
untruthfulness and deception. To develop,
use the following Auto-Suggestion: "John
Smith, you are learning to keep your own secrets; you are learning the art of keeping
your mouth closed and your tongue quiet; you
are learning that "a closed mouth catches no
flies," and are acting accordingly; you are
developing the faculty of holding your tongue,
and to avoid "blabbing" your secrets to the
world; you are becoming reticent and self-
contained; you are avoiding wearing your
heart on your' sleeve, or of exhibiting your
open wounds that the world may stick its
finger into them; you are learning to "lay

low, and keep dark;'' you are learning to ''saw wood and say nothing;'' you are learning to set the watch-dog of your caution at the door of your mind, so as to prevent others from entering; you are developing the quality of being guarded and wary; you are becoming reserved and cautious; you are avoiding the role of the fool who tells all he knows, for the secret amusement and benefit of others; you are avoiding all gushing and emotional slushiness; you are learning to dwell within your own mental castle, and gazing through your windows at the world, without inviting them to occupy the inner chambers of your soul. You are inside your own castle, and have locked the door,'' etc. Accompany this with the appropriate ideal and mental picture, and *make good in action.* *Be* secretive, as well as saying you are. Let your thought take form in action.

The above should give you an idea of the method to be applied in the development of any faculty. Apply the same method in developing the other faculties mentioned below, and any others that may seem desirable to you. There is no secret in the words. Model your Auto-Suggestion in accordance with the characteristics of each faculty as given below, and you can make your own Auto-Suggestions.

5. *Approbativeness.* This is the faculty which causes us to feel hurt when we are condemned by others; and to feel exalted when others flatter or "jolly" us. The majority of us have too much of this quality, and restraint, rather than development is necessary in most cases. The best way to restrain this faculty is to cultivate the spirit of Individuality and true Self-Esteem. Learn to feel: "They say; what do they say; let them say!" Learn to stand on your own feet, and smile at the world. Learn to say "I Am," and feel that you are surrounded with a protective atmosphere of individual strength, through which the adverse criticism cannot reach you. At the same time, learn to be proof against flattery and the false praise of others. Learn to value your own satisfaction as more than the praise of the world. Learn to live in spite of condemnation or adverse criticism; and without the flattery of knaves, fools, and self-seeking people.

6. *Self-Esteem.* True Self-Esteem consists in the feeling of Individuality, as distinct from Personality. Personality is the
phase of the self which is affected by criticism
or flattery—its organ is Approbativeness.
The true individual feels that he is *real*—that
he is a centre of the cosmic energy—that he
is standing on his own feet, and is a necessary
part of the world's being. Self-Esteem does
not display Egotism, for that fault belongs to
the personality. Self-Esteem is Egoistic
but not Egotistic—there is a world of difference between these terms. Cultivate the "I
Am" quality within yourself—develop the individuality. "I Am an Individual" is the
key note of true Self-Esteem.

7. *Firmness.* This is the faculty of
steadfastness, stability, perseverance, decision, tenacity, will. It may be cultivated by
the methods given above. The qualities of
firmness, its ideal, its actions, are too well
known to require a recital.

Hope—the faculty of optimism, expectation of good, bright outlook, etc.; Construc-
tiveness, the faculty of "making things"—the
inventive faculty; and many other positive

qualities, may be cultivated by the methods already given. In suggesting these qualities to yourself, use the same words and terms that you would use were you suggesting to another person. By keeping this rule in mind, you should have no trouble in selecting the appropriate suggestions.

The qualities and faculties given above are for the most part what are known as The Positive Qualities, and are those in which the majority of people are deficient. For this reason we have placed special emphasis upon them. There are other valuable qualities, necessary in a well-rounded character, but we have thought it best to emphasize these Positive Qualities for the reason that the lack of development of them has resulted in so many weak characters, and that the work should be directed to the point of the greatest need. In conclusion, we ask you to consider these words used by us in concluding a previous work, in which the spirit of the Positive Qualities is brought out: "I have tried to infuse my words with the strong, vital energy, which I feel surging through me as I write out this message of strength to you. I trust that these words will act as a current

of verbal electrons, each carrying its full
charge of dynamic power. And I trust that
each word will serve to fill you with the mind-
power that gave them birth, and will thus
awaken in you a similar mental state, desire
and will, to be strong, forceful and dynamic—
determined to assert your individuality in being and doing that which the universal crea-
tive desire and will is hoping that you will be
and do. I send to you this message, charged
with the very dynamic vibrations of my brain,
as it transforms and converts the mind-power
into thoughts and words. I send it to you—
yes, *you,* who are now reading the words—
with all the energy, force and power at my
command, to the end that it pierce your armor
of indifference, fear and doubt, and 'I Can't.'
And that reaching your heart of desire, it
may fill you with the very spirit of individuality, conscious egohood, perception of reality,
and realization of the 'I.' So that from now
on your battle cry will be changed, and you
will plunge into the thick of the fight, filled
with the Berserker rage, like the Icelandic
hero of old, and shouting your positive cry of
freedom: 'I Can and I Will!' you will mow

your way clear through the ranks of the hordes of ignorance, and negativity, and reach the heights beyond. This is my message to *you*—the Individual!"

CHAPTER XX.

In the words used as the title for this concluding chapter—Health, Happiness and Prosperity—are summed up the majority of the things which render life worth living, and for which mankind is striving. And if Auto-Suggestion tends to develop these qualities or states, then it plays a most important part in the life of mankind. And all students of the subject are forced to concede that Auto-Suggestion has much to do with Health, Happiness and Prosperity, either in the direction of producing them, or of preventing them. Let us give a brief final consideration to the subject of Auto-Suggestion in its effect of the Health, Happiness and Prosperity of men and women.

In the first place, we have seen the therapeutic value of Suggestion, in its various phases. And we have seen that each and every effect of Therapeutic Suggestion really has Auto-Suggestion as its fundamental principle, for, at the last, the healing power of Suggestion is found to reside in the mind of the individual, himself, and that all of its activities arise from the calling into effect of the mental power of the person by Auto-Suggestion, conscious or unconscious. And every form of Therapeutic Suggestion mentioned in this book as employed by the various practitioners, may be applied by the person himself, to himself, by Auto-Suggestion. We have explained how one may suggest to himself, with the same effect as if he were suggesting to another. In this way the whole system of Suggestive Therapeutics is open to each and every person, without the aid of a healer or practitioner, if he has the perseverance and will to so apply it.

Moreover, the careful reader of this book will have seen that one's health depends materially upon the character of his mental states—that the mind exerts a tremendous influence over the physical states. He will have seen that the influence of Fear, Worry, Anger and gloomy mental states are actually depressing in their effects upon the functions of the bodily organs. And that Hope, Faith,

Courage and Cheerfulness exert a positive, invigorating effect upon the physical functions. This being the case, does it not follow that a habit of proper Auto-Suggestion once acquired and practiced, the person must of necessity interpose a resistance to disease, and develop a normal, healthy condition of physical life. Read over carefully what we have said in the part of this book devoted to Therapeutic Suggestion, and then apply the principles along the lines of Auto-Suggestion. Proper Auto-Suggestion comes as near to being a universal remedy for disease, as anything ever known to man. That is, Auto-Suggestion accompanied by the proper ideals and mental pictures, and the manifestation in action, as described in this book. If you *suggest* Health to yourself; *think* Health; *see* Health; and *act* Health—you will *manifest* Health. *Let your ideal, model and pattern always be the Healthy Man or Woman, and then model all your suggestions, thoughts and actions accordingly.*

As for Happiness, much depends upon the possession of Health. And the first step in the acquisition of Happiness is the development of Health. But, in addition to this the Mental Attitude of persons depend very materially upon the principle of Auto-Suggestion and the will. By steadily refusing to allow the entrance of depressing negative thoughts, and the constant seeking for the positive, invigorating thoughts, you have the key of the proper Mental Attitude. "As a man thinketh, so is he." Man grows to resemble that upon which he fixes his thoughts. A determination to see and think of only the positive bright things of life, and the refusal to admit or consider the negative, depressing things of life, will produce a habitual mental attitude which will make for Happiness. There are both bright and dark things in life, but we have the right to turn our attention to which ever set of facts and things we desire. We may prefer to see only the unpleasant side and many seemingly so prefer; or we may prefer to see only the bright side. It is all a matter of determination and will, along the lines of using the attention. The attention finds that which it seeks, good or bad. There are always two sides to everything—you have the right to choose which side you will gaze upon. Optimism and Pessimism are but the two sides of the Shield of Life—take your choice. Much depends upon the Mental Attitude, and the Mental Attitude depends largely upon Auto-Suggestion, in its fullest sense.

Happiness is not so much a matter of outside things as is generally imagined. You have seen many persons surrounded by all that wealth, position, or influence could procure—and still they are unhappy. On the contrary, you have seen many people like "Mrs Wiggs of the Cabbage Patch," or like "Glad" in "The Dawn of a Tomorrow," who manage to extract Happiness from the must unpromising surroundings. Happiness comes from *within*. If you are not able to extract it from within your soul, you will never get it from without. It is something that belongs to the inner nature of people—it exists nowhere else. No one ever obtained perfect happiness from outside things, people, or conditions—but many have found it dwelling within themselves. And, so, if you cultivate your "within" you have found the secret of happiness. And the "within" may be developed and cultivated by Auto-Suggestion, as we have defined the word. You live in your mind, after all—therefore you should make your mental dwelling-place fit to live in.

Prosperity depends upon a number of things, not the least of which is the inner mental attitude and condition of those seeking it. The possession of certain qualities of mind is generally regarded as necessary for Success; and the possession of opposite qualities are generally regarded as destructive to Success. If ones mental faculties or qualities were fixed and unalterable, then one might despair of attaining Success, in the majority of cases. But The New Psychology has shown us how we may develop desirable qualities, and restrain undesirable ones, by Auto-Suggestion. So we see that even in this field, Auto-Suggestion plays an important part.

All improvement comes by education in some form. Auto-Suggestion is simply a form of education and training. The fact that you are both teacher and student, does not alter the question. A recognition of the existence of the subconscious mind explains the dual-action in Auto-Suggestion. One has it within his own power *to make of himself what he will,* providing he will devote to the task energy, determination and persistency. And even these qualities may be developed and encouraged, if one be deficient in them.

There is a "Something Within" each person that is the King and Master of all the remaining portions of his being. Call this "something within" the soul, the will, the ego, or what not, the fact remains that this part of the self is Sovereign and Dominant. In the measure that this Sovereign manifests its power, so is the degree of Individuality. The majority of people do not realize that they have this Sovereign Self within them, and so yield themselves without resistance to environment and outward influences. In Auto-Suggestion, particularly when one acquires the "knack" of it, there is manifested the phenomenon of this Sovereign Self mounting its mental throne and asserting its right and might to govern. Then does man become the master of himself, instead of being a slave to circumstance and environment, or the influence of others. In the realization, recognition and manifestation of this "I Am" within us, lies the secret of Health, Happiness and Prosperity. As Chas. F. Lummis has said: "Man was meant to be, and ought to be, stronger and more than anything that can happen to him. Circumstances, 'fate,' 'luck' are all outside, and if he cannot always change them, *he can always beat them*. . . . I am all right. I am bigger than anything that can happen to me. All these things are outside my door, *and I've got the key*." And so say all who have found the "something within," and have gained the Mastery of Self by Self!

FINIS.

COSIMO is a specialty publisher of books and publications that inspire, inform, and engage readers. Our mission is to offer unique books to niche audiences around the world.

COSIMO BOOKS publishes books and publications for innovative authors, nonprofit organizations, and businesses. **COSIMO BOOKS** specializes in bringing books back into print, publishing new books quickly and effectively, and making these publications available to readers around the world.

COSIMO CLASSICS offers a collection of distinctive titles by the great authors and thinkers throughout the ages. At **COSIMO CLASSICS** timeless works find new life as affordable books, covering a variety of subjects including: Business, Economics, History, Personal Development, Philosophy, Religion & Spirituality, and much more!

COSIMO REPORTS publishes public reports that affect your world, from global trends to the economy, and from health to geopolitics.